# Reviews from Kelly's Other Books

I am excited for Kelly's book to bring healing and hope to others. Many times we create in our own victories, the keys that help others find what they are looking for. I pray for you to find what you need in these pages.

—Danny Silk
Leader at Bethel Church, Redding, CA
President of Loving On Purpose, Inc.
Author of *Culture of Honor*

Kelly Ann Evers knows from experience that just getting away from one's abuser doesn't stop the pain. *Dynamic Prayers, Changed Lives* are an excellent resource for women caught in abusive relationships. Evers talks straight with victims of abuse. She helps the reader "call it what it is" and identify when she's in an abusive relationship. There are practical checklists for preparing to leave safely, guided prayers that connect the reader with the protection and peace of God, and specific studies in the Bible to complete the journey to healing that is only started by the act of leaving. Get this book into the hands of any victimized woman. It very well could save her life.

—Shelley Leith
Co-Author, *Character Makeover*

*Hurt No More (Dynamic Prayers, Changed Lives)* will be a wonderful help to those who have suffered from abuse. I highly recommend this book to you.

—Dr. Mark Virkler
—*Prayers That Heal the Heart*
WWW.CWGMinistries.org

As strange as it may seem, victims are not always aware that they are living in an abusive situation. They may be convinced falsely that they are to blame, or the abuse has occurred for so many years, they have come to believe this is normal. Kelly Ann Evers points out warning signs and gives insight into recognizing various types of abuse, including emotional, physical, sexual, spiritual, and economic. Her book extends hope and provides resources for the healing journey.

—PatsyLewis
Author of *Simply Praying* and *Simply Listening*
www.patsyspottersclayministry.com

In *Dynamic Prayers Changed Lives,* Kelly Ann Evers focuses on what has become a crisis in the United States and other countries—the prevalence of Domestic Violence. When Kelly found the courage to leave her abusive husband 16 years ago, there were very few resources available to help her and other women. It became her mission to change this. Today, she is the founder of His Love Heals, Domestic Violence Help, and is a highly respected international authority on domestic violence. In this book, Kelly has written about her own life-changing journey, her successful healing, and provides abused women important information and effective tools to help them leave their abusive relationships, and eventually attain the happy and fulfilling lives they deserve.

—D. S. Bryan
Consumer Advocate
Health and Education Research Consultant

Kelly inspires and entices as she walks you to the breakfast table with the Lord, at the foot of the Cross, for the greatest gift of healing and relationship. I've worn the edges and corners down waiting and wanting more time to sit with Kelly and the Lord through… You will have a hard time putting this book down!

—Pam Murray
Founder of Surviving Domestic Violence

*Dynamic Prayers, Changed Lives: One Woman's Journey of Healing from Abuse through Prayer and the Word of God is* never leaving my bedside as the prayers and Scripture soothe me…  I could relate to Kelly's voice, her writing, and most of all, could feel God working in me as we explored healing together through His love.  The prayers are life-changing, spirit lifting, and an amazing comfort in all stages of healing.

—Erin Al-Mehairi
Hook of a Book Reviews

Kelly Ann Evers is one of the most charming, warm, loving people you will ever meet! She has a true pastor's heart; she cares deeply for women and their welfare. As an abuse survivor herself, she is passionate about helping other abuse victims get the help and healing they need. Kelly is truly a woman after God's own heart. She has an incredible personal relationship with Jesus, and she draws her strength, wisdom, and inspiration from Him daily. Her humility, prayerfulness, and outstanding character make her an invaluable source of spiritual and practical help for anyone going through abuse. I am privileged to have her as a friend.

Mike and Norma Letinsky,
Kingdom Partners, CA.

# God's Word on Domestic Violence
## Scriptures Only Edition
### Series 2

**4TH EDITION IN PRINT**

# One Thousand Scriptures on Abuse
# And How God Responds
# … because love should never hurt!

Discover God's ZERO Tolerance towards Domestic Violence and
How He RESPONDS to It!

# KELLY ANN EVERS

———————————————

Founder of His Love Heals, Domestic Violence Help

v

Scripture Only God's Word on Domestic Violence: One Thousand Scriptures on Abuse and How God Responds to It … because love should never hurt! Discover God's ZERO Tolerance towards Domestic Violence and How He RESPONDS to It! 4TH Edition

Library of Congress Cataloging-in-Publication Data

Evers, Kelly Ann.

God's Word on Domestic Violence: One Thousand Scriptures: Scripture Only Edition, because love should never hurt! Discover God's ZERO Tolerance towards Domestic Violence and How He RESPONDS to It! / Kelly Ann Evers. 4th Edition in Print

p. cm.
ISBN: 9798729005994

1. Abused women.   2. Spiritual life.   3. Evers,
Kelly Ann. I. Title.
HV6626.E94   2021   362.82 92 '
QBI11-600102

Please note that Life Journey Publishing™ style capitalizes certain pronouns in Scripture that refer to the Father, Son, and Holy Spirit, and may differ from some publishers' styles. Internet addresses printed in this book are offered as a resource to you. These are not intended in any way to be or imply an endorsement on the part of Life Journey Publishing™, nor do we vouch for the content of these sites and number for the life of this book. This book is sold with the understanding that neither the author nor publisher is engaged in rendering any legal or psychological advice. The author and publisher disclaim any personal liability, directly or indirectly, for advice or information presented within.

## Proudly Printed in the United States of America

# Foreword

## *MIRROR, MIRROR©*

By Rebekah Walker

Mirror, Mirror on the wall,
I'm not the fairest one of all.

I look at you and all I see, Are
scars and fears in front of me.

Not a beauty, and not a queen,
Living in the shadows of life it seems.

A girl forgotten and unloved,
Been bruised and beaten, pushed and shoved.

How are some girls worth fighting for…
While I'm all alone…bleeding on the floor.

God, where are you?!
Rescue me! I cried
aloud, and He came to
me.

I looked in the mirror and saw
Him there, He held me and told
me how much He cares.

He let me know I'm not alone,
He called me His princess, an heir to the throne.

He touched my heart and healed
my wounds, I traded it in for His
sweet perfume.

Mirror, Mirror now I see,
The lovely woman He's called me to be.

His love and goodness, they changed
my heart, He erased my past and gave
me a fresh start.

"The Lord is near to the brokenhearted and saves the
crushed in spirit." Psalm 34:18

# Table of Contents

# God Promises You

Did you know that the Bible is a promise to you? When we pray God's Word over our lives and the lives of others, His power is unleashed to meet our needs. You cannot pray wrong when you speak the Word of God over yourself.

As you begin to read the Scriptures in this book, you can pray the Scripture over yourself or slightly paraphrase it. Each Scripture regarding domestic violence and abuse is God's promise to you.

As we spend time praying these Scriptures over ourselves, meditating on them, and believing they will change our lives, something happens within our spirit. The truth of God's Word brings us a sudden boost of hope, more faith, courage, and confidence. We begin to feel the actual depth of God's love for us. And we immediately experience peace.

Knowing that God has zero tolerance for domestic violence empowers us to make vital changes in our lives. They help us see that when you are hurting, God hurts also. All abuse and violence done against you breaks God's heart.

God's Word is not just His promise to us. It is also His love letter to us. Every time you read or think about the prayers and Scriptures in this book, ask God to show you His love through these prayers and Scriptures. Ask Him to give you a greater understanding of His love, and ask Him to remove anything that could block you from receiving His love.

Prayer is an essential component of our lives. Without prayer, we cannot become close to God. And without prayer, answers don't come to us. Should I say that again? Without prayer, answers don't come to us.

James 4:2b says, "Yet the reason you don't have what you want is that you don't ask God for it (NLT)." If you want something from God just ask! It's that simple. We need to pray, we need to ask, and we need to keep praying and asking until we have our answer. "The earnest prayer of a righteous person has great power and pro- duces wonderful results ( James 5:16b NLT)."

I strongly believe there is an anointing on this book. Whenever you feel discouraged, depressed, unloved, fearful—the moment life becomes difficult for you—find Scriptures in this book that relate to your situation, and then pray them over yourself. I promise you will experience immediate relief. You will be lifted out of despair, and will have hope again.

We can trust in God's Word. He keeps His promises to us and He will never let you down. He wants nothing more than for you to stop hurting. So are you ready to see miracles happen? Are you ready to see God's Word change your life? Yes? Then let's pray and meditate on these Scriptures!

# Trusting God's Word

Romans 12:12 tells us to renew our mind. This is the basis of this book. Understanding what Scripture says about abuse, God's zero tolerance for it, and meditating on them enables us to renew our mind.

The renewing of our minds doesn't just add to the already completed work of Jesus Christ. It simply puts us in a mental state that enables us to better use our faith. That helps us enjoy the benefits of the redemptive work of Jesus.

God is so good. He wants only the best for you. Really.

So many times, we think that God doesn't care, and if He did, He would cure us, heal us, deliver us, or take the pain away.

I wish I could have a clear-cut answer for God, but I don't. But what I do have is hope and trust in what He promises me and you.

He does promise that He will heal our broken heart, heal us from our distresses, remove us from abusive relationships, and wipe our tears.  He promises us that though we walk in a dark season of pain and suffering, He will carry us.  He says that He will stand beside you and walk you on the right path.

To be clear, when God's says He will remove us from our batterers, we have to do our part.  Which is preparing to leave, having an escape plan, having emergency numbers and so forth.  For a complete planning guide my book:

"Creating Your Personal Safety Planning Kit and Domestic Violence Emergency Prep-kit"

I'll be the first person who will say, "God why not just wave a magic wand and miraculously move me to a safe house?" You have to prepare and find the strength to take the next step.  It's not easy, but when you do get out, you will feel like the world is yours.  You'll feel like "Superwoman" ready to climb over every obstacle.

Although I don't see it every day, I know what He says is true.  I have seen Him come through for me thousands of times.

One thing I've learned is that we are not exempt from problems. We live in the world just like everyone else. We shop at the same grocery stores, eat at the same restaurants, fold laundry, go to work and cook dinner like the rest of the world.

The difference is that we don't do it alone. So when we are shopping, we invite God on our shopping spree, we invite Him to help us make choices, and if we walk out to our car and someone dings our car, we ask God to help us forgive the person.

We aren't immune from problems; we just have the privilege to have a God who helps us "survive" our difficulties.

That's where these healing Scriptures come in. Knowing that everyone faces difficulties, we know we are not alone. There is something comforting knowing others face problems just like ours, plus, we are comforted that God is there with us carrying us and helping us live our life to the fullest!

Did you know God has a "wish list" for us? He wishes, desires and longs for us to have everything He has promised in His Word.

There are over 30,000 promises in the Bible and all of them are for you!  He wants to see you prosper and be successful in every part of your life.  Not just some, but all areas!

When we declare His Word, God starts working in our lives. Isaiah 55:11-12 (NLT) says, "It is the same with My Word. I send it out, and it always produces fruit.  It will accomplish all I want it to, and it will prosper everywhere I send it.  You will live in joy and peace." When we declare and pray His Word over our lives and others, He says He will make it happen – guaranteed!

**Take a Look at the Scriptures in Isaiah:**

Isaiah 30:18 (NASB) says, "Therefore the Lord longs to be gracious to you, and therefore He waits on high to have compassion on you.  For the Lord is a God of justice; how bless are all those who long for Him."

Isaiah 30:18 (Amplified) says, "And the Lord [earnestly] waits [expecting, looking, and longing] to be gracious to you; and therefore, He lifts Himself up, that He may have mercy on you and show loving-kindness to you.  For the Lord is a God of justice.  Blessed (happy, fortunate, to be envied) are all those who [earnestly] wait for Him, who expects and look and long for Him [for His victory, His favor, His love, His peace, His joy, and His matchless, unbroken companionship]!" (See John 14:3, 27; 2 Cor. 12:9; Heb. 12:2; 1 John 3:16 for more like this Scripture).

I love reading it in the Amplified version because it says God earnestly waits, looks, longs, and expects to bless us.  When I read it, I get this picture of God sitting on the edge of the seat, on His throne, waiting with anticipation to just bless us.

 I can see Him huddling with His angels saying: "Angel John you go do this because that is what she has asked for, and Angel Samantha you do that, because I just want to bless her, and Angel Tabatha go do this because I want to see her smile again."  I think God gets giddy when He is about to bless and answer our prayers and declarations!

No matter how difficult your situation is right now, no matter how big it is, no matter how dangerous it is, no matter how impossible it seems, God promises that His Word is true and it will come to pass.

My success came when I began praying and declaring the Scriptures over my life and each circumstance.  When I was going through something difficult, I found Scriptures that pertained to that subject and I prayed them, declared "it is written" and I read them many times throughout the day.

I found success because I crushed the devil and his evil assaults against me with the Word of God.  I found my freedom because I was determined to receive all of what God promised me.

**God Answered My Prayers.**

I was delivered, healed, restored and experienced peace in the most devastating times of my life because His Word gave me peace and hope.

**I Didn't Give Up Praying His Word, Until I Got the Answers I Wanted.**

This is your answer too. If you want freedom from the pain, depression, hopelessness, abuse and so forth you have to stand on God's Word daily – sometimes hourly.

Think about it this way: if you go to the doctor and he prescribes you medicine to take 4 times daily for 4 weeks, you take it right?

If man-made medicine is helpful, how much more is God's Word? If you are desperate enough to see changes in your life than let me prescribe to you a heavenly RX. Find Scriptures in this book that pertain to your situation you are currently facing write them out on 3x5 cards and read each verse three times, four times a day – out loud.

Start off by thanking God for His promise, and then read the Scripture.

Second, declare to the devil God's promise, by saying "devil God's Word says, _______________ (reading that same Scripture again).

Then tell yourself, I declare and I believe I will receive _______________ (by saying the same Scripture once again).

I did this for myself many times (maybe 100's of times) for different situations.  Each time I found victory in all my situations.

The key though, is to be consistent and persistent.  It's easy to forget to do it, life gets in the way, problems arise and the day passes us but if you are serious about having victory in your life and follow my prescription, you'll see miracles unfold!

Set an alarm on your phone, have your computer remind you, do whatever it takes to remember to declare these Scriptures.

Tape them on the mirror in the bathroom. Recite them while getting ready.  Record them on your phone and listen to them on your way to work, or in the background while working.

And those times you don't feel like doing it, that is the devil trying to thwart your promises to coming to pass – when that happens, declare double the number of Scriptures!  Beat the devil at his own game – crush him and stop him from stealing from you.

# One Thousand Scriptures

# Anxiety

He will not fail you or leave you (Deuteronomy 31:6 ERV).

He hath delivered my soul in peace from the battle that was sent against me… (Psalm 55:18 KJV).

I am praying in my time of trouble.  I know you will answer me (Psalm 86:7 ERV).

Thou wilt keep him in perfect peace, whose mind is stayed on Thee: because he trusts in Thee (Isaiah 26:3 KJV).

[The Cure for Anxiety] "For this reason I say to you, do not be worried about your life, as to what you will eat or what you will drink; nor for your body, as to what you will put on. Is not life more than food, and the body more than clothing… (Matthew 6:25 NASB)?

And don't worry about food – what to eat and drink. Don't worry whether God will provide it for you.  These things dominate the thoughts of most people, but your Father already knows your needs.  He will give you all you need from day to day if you make the Kingdom of God your primary concern.  "So don't be afraid, little flock. For it gives your Father great happiness to give you the Kingdom (Luke 12:29-32 NASB).

And because you belong to Christ Jesus, God's peace will stand guard over all your thoughts and feelings.  His peace can do this far better than our human minds (Philippians 4:7 ERV).

The Spirit God does not make us afraid.  His Spirit is a source of power and love and self-control (2 Timothy 1:7 ERV).

Give all your worries to Him, because He cares for you (1 Peter 5:7 ERV).

Anxiety in a man's heart weighs him down, but a good word makes him glad (Proverbs 12:25).

A joyful heart makes a cheerful countenance, but sorrow of the heart crushes the spirit.  (Proverbs 15:13).

The Lord God has given me the tongue of discipleship, to sustain the weary with a word.  He awakens me morning by morning; He awakens my ear to listen as a disciple (Isaiah 50:4).

A merry heart does good like medicine; but a broken spirit dries the bones (Proverbs 17:22).

# Bible Verses about Love

For God so loved the world that He gave His only Son, so that everyone who believes in Him will not perish but have eternal life (John 3:16 NLT).

For the Lord delights in you and will claim you as His own (Isaiah 62:4b NLT).

Long ago the Lord has said, "I have loved you, my people, with an everlasting love.  With unfailing love I have drawn you to myself… You again will be happy and dance merrily with tambourines (Jeremiah 31:3 NLT).

We pray that the Lord Jesus Christ Himself and God our Father will comfort you and strengthen you in every good thing you do and say.  God loved us and gave us through grace a wonderful hope and comfort that has no end (2 Thessalonians 2:16-17 ERV).

Give thanks to the God of gods, for His steadfast love endures forever.  Give thanks to the God of gods for His gracious love is everlasting (Psalm 136:2).

God loves us and we have put our trust in His Love (1 John 4:16).

God loves you (Deuteronomy 23:5)

I have loved you, says the Lord.  (Malachi 1:2).

# More Bible Verses about Love

The Lord your God is with you and how happy He is with you.  He will laugh and be happy about you, like people at a party (Zephaniah 3:17 ERV).

I will show them My love without limits (Hosea 14:4b).

He loves those who try to do good (Proverbs 15:9).

But God so rich in His mercy, and He loved us so very much, that even while we were dead because of our own sins, He gave us life when He raised Christ from the dead.  (It is only by God's special favor that you have been saved!) For He raised us from the dead along with Christ, and we are seated with Him in the heavenly realms—all because we are one with Christ Jesus.  And so God can always point to us as examples of the incredible wealth of His favor and kindness toward us, as shown in all He has done for us through Christ Jesus (Ephesian 2:4-7 NLT).

God saved you by His special favor when you believed. And you can't take credit for this; it is a gift from God. Salvation is not a reward for the good things we have done, so none of us can boast about it. For we are God's masterpiece. He has created us anew in Christ Jesus, so that we can do the good things He planned for us so long ago (Ephesians 2:8 NLT).

God showed how much He loved us by sending His only Son into the world so that we might have eternal life through Him. This is real love. It is not that we loved God, but that He loved us and sent His Son as a sacrifice to take away our sins (1 John 4:9-10 NLT).

And I am convinced that nothing can ever separate us from His love. Death can't, and life can't. The angels can't and the demons can't. Our fears for today; our worries about tomorrow, and even the powers of hell can't keep God's love away. Whether we are high above the sky or in the deepest ocean, nothing in all creation will ever be able to separate us from the love of God that is reveals in Christ Jesus our Lord (Romans 8:38-39 NLT).

None of this fazes us because Jesus loves us. I am absolutely convinced that nothing—nothing living or dead, angelic or demonic, today or tomorrow, high or low, thinkable or unthinkable—absolutely nothing can get between us and God's love because of the way that Jesus our Master has embraced us (Romans 8:38-39 Message).

The Father Himself loves you dearly because you love Me (Jesus) and believe that I came from God (John 16:27).

I will be in them, and You will be in Me.  So they will be completely one. Then the world will know that You sent Me and that You loved them just as You loved Me  (John 17:23 ERV).

We know this because God has poured out His love to fill our hearts through the Holy Spirit, He gave us (Romans 5:5).

Can anything separate us from Christ's love? Can trouble or problems or persecution separate us from His love?  If we have no food or clothing or face danger or even death, will that separate us from His love?  As the Scriptures says, "for we are in danger of death all the time.  People think we are worth no more than sheep to be killed." But in all these troubles we have complete victory through God, who has shown his love for us.  Yes, I am sure that nothing can separate us from God's love—not death, life, angels, or ruling spirits.  I am sure that nothing now, nothing in the future, no powers, nothing above us or nothing below us— nothing in the whole created world—will ever be able to separate us in Christ Jesus our Lord (Romans 8:35-38 ERV).

# Confidence

Be determined and confident. Do not be afraid of them. Your God, the Lord himself, will be with you. He will not fail you or abandon you (Deuteronomy 31:6 GNT).

I am strong and courageous!  I will not be afraid or discouraged. For the Lord my God is with me wherever I go (Joshua 1:9 paraphrased).

You will be confident, because there is hope. You will look carefully about and lie down in safety (Job 11:18 CSB).

In Your strength I can crush any army; with my God I can scale a wall (Psalm 18:29 paraphrased).

Though an army besiege me, my heart will not fear; though war break out against me, even then will I be confident (Psalm 27:3 NIV).

Though a mighty army surrounds me, my heart will know no fear. Even if they attack me, I remain confident (Psalm 27:3 NLT).

I am still confident of this: I will see the goodness of the LORD in the land of the living (Psalm 27:13 NLT).

I trust in the Lord and do good.  Therefore, I will live safely in the land and prosper (Psalm 37:3-5 paraphrased).

My heart is confident in you, O God; no wonder I can sing your praises (Psalm 57:7 NLT)!

I am confident and fearless and can face my foes triumphantly (Psalm 112:8 paraphrased)!

Strength and honor are her clothing; she is confident about the future (Proverbs 31:25 CEB).

We are confident of all this because of our great trust in God through Christ (2 Corinthians 3:4 NLT).

# *Court*

*Kelly here…I wanted to share with you my experiences with these court Scriptures.  When my divorce started I started going through the Bible to find Scriptures about court, what God said about my abuser lying in court and every possible situation I would experience.  (Remember, the internet was barely around then. So I had to actually read the Bible to find these ☺) If you are going to go to court bring this book with you.  Or purchase the "A Thousand Scriptures: Scriptures Only" or "Another Thousand Scriptures on Domestic Violence."  Have it in a soft cover book so the judge doesn't think you're playing on the internet.  And as you're hearing the lies, the hurtful words, and everything else that is happening, meditate on these Scriptures.  This was the only way I was able to withstand the pain and sorrow I was experiencing in court.*

*At the time, I brought in a hand written spiral bound notebook with all these Scriptures.  We had A LOT of court appearances.  By the end of a 4-year divorce, the notebook was so tear stained that most of it was illegible.  But after 4 years, I had them all memorized!  This book is going to be your best friend, when everything feels like it's falling apart and when it feels like your ex is winning in court.  Just know God is with you, always!*

The Sovereign Lord will wipe away all tears.  He will remove forever all insults and mockery against His land and people.  The Lord has spoken (Isaiah 25:8 ERV).

God, you showed that I was innocent.  You gave me relief from all my troubles (Psalm 4:1).

You destroy those who tells lies.  Lord, you hate those who make secret plans to hurt others (Psalm 5:6).

Take your place on the bench, reach for your gavel, throw out the false charges against me. I'm ready, confident in your verdict: "Innocent" (Psalm 7:8 MSG).

God helps people who want to do right, so He will protect me.  God is a good judge.  He always condemns evil (Psalm 7:10-11)

Some people are just troublemakers.  They are always thinking up some crooked plan and telling lies.  They will use secret signals to cheat people; they will wink their eye, shuffle their feet and point a finger.  They are always planning to do something bad.  But they will be punished.  Disaster will strike, and they will be destroyed.  There will be no one to help them (Proverbs 6:12-15).

The Lord hates these seven things:  eyes that show pride, tongues that tells lies, hands that kill innocent people, hearts that planed evil things to do, feet that run to do evil, witnesses in court who tell lies, and anyone who causes family members to fight (Proverbs 16-19 ERV).

A witness who lies will be punished; that liar will not escape (Proverbs 19:5).

A witness who lies will be punished.  That liar will be destroyed (Proverbs 19:9).

But He will argue my case for me in court.  He will do what is right for me (Micah 7:9).

Everything that is hidden will be shown.  Everything that is secret will be made known (Matthew 10:26).

*Although your abuser is lying in court, God will reveal the truth. Those lies will be made known to the judge!*  Another verse says:

Everything that is hidden will become clear. Every secret thing will be made known and everyone will see it (Luke 8:17 ERV).

*As you face court issues, your abuser will accuse you of all sorts of things, he will say you are not a good mother, you are an abuser.  But trust the Lord and His Word.  God promises you that those lies will be revealed and the truth will be known.*  Another verse says:

Everything that is hidden will be shown, and everything that is secret will be made known.  What you say in dark will be told in the light.  And what you whisper in a private room will be shouted from the housetop (Luke 12:2 ERV).

*In Genesis God says that when He says something twice, expect it to be done... how much more should you expect immediate relief if it's said 3 times?  When you read those Scriptures above you know God is very serious about lying in court, and He will not let anyone get by with it.*

*When people are hurting you and abusing you God is not with them and they will be defeated! This is God's promise to you:*

The Lord is not with you (those abusing you), and your enemies will defeat you (Numbers 14:42 GNT, comment mine).

# Court: Good Scriptures for Experiencing Peace in Court

O God who declares me innocent.  Take away my distress. Have mercy on me and hear my prayer (Psalm 4:1 NLT).

Lord, You know the hopes of the helpless.  Surely You will listen to their cries and comfort them.  You will bring justice to the orphans and the oppressed, so people can no longer terrify them (Psalm 10:17-18 NLT).

I trust in the Lord for protection (Psalm 11:1 NLT).

O Lord, hear my plea for justice, listen to my cry for help. Pay attention to my prayer, for it comes from an honest heart. Declare me innocent, for you know those who do right (Psalm 17:1-2 NLT).

Wake up!  Rise to my defense!  Take up my case, my God and my Lord.  Declare me "not guilty," O Lord my God, for you give justice (Psalm 35:23-24 NLT).

O God, take up my cause!  Defend me against these ungodly people.  Rescue me from these unjust liars (Psalm 43:1 NLT).

You will restore me to even greater honor and comfort me once again (Psalm 71:21 NLT).

The Lord gives righteousness and justice to all who are treated unfairly (Psalm 103:6 NLT).

The humble will be filled with fresh joy from the Lord. Those who are poor will rejoice in the Holy One of Israel. Those who intimidate and harass will be gone, and all those who plot evil will be killed.  Those who make the innocent guilty by their false testimony will disappear.  And those how use trickery to pervert justice and tell lies to tear down the innocent will be no more (Isaiah 29:19-21 NLT).

He will bring full justice to all who have been wronged.  He will not stop until truth and righteousness prevail… (Isaiah 42:3-4 NLT).


I will give you treasures hidden in the darkness – secret riches (Isaiah 45:3).


But forget all that—it is nothing compared to what I am going to do.  For I am about to do a brand-new thing.  See, I have already begun!  Do you not see it?  I will make a pathway through the wilderness for my people to come home, I will create rivers for them in the desert.  …Yes, I will make springs in the desert, so that my chosen people can be refreshed (Isaiah 43:18-20).


I have said it: I am calling Cyrus!  I will send him on this errand and will help him succeed.  Come closer and listen.  I have always told you plainly what would happen so you would have no trouble understanding (Isaiah 48:15).


…He never lets the guilty go unpunished (Nahum 1:3b NLT).


For I will fight those who fight you, and I will save your children (Isaiah 49:25b).

And everyone who tells lies in court will be brought to justice.  These benefits are enjoyed of the Lord; their vindication will come from Me.  I, the Lord, have spoken! (Isaiah 54:17 NLT).

For I, the Lord, love justice.  I hate robbery and wrongdoing.  I will faithfully reward my people for their suffering and make an everlasting covenant with them (Isaiah 61:8 NLT).

I will give you back your health and heal your wounds, says the Lord (Jeremiah 30:17 NLT).

Lord, You are my lawyer!  Plead my case!  For you have redeemed my life.  You have seen the wrong they have done, Lord.  Be my judge, and prove me right (Lamentations 3:58-59 NLT).

# *Court*

Pray over the judge, jury, attorneys, defendant, respondent and anyone else apart of the court hearing

And the Spirit of the Lord will rest on him – the Spirit of wisdom and understanding, the Spirit of counsel and might, the Spirit of knowledge and the fear of the Lord.  He will delight in obeying the Lord (Isaiah 11:2-3b NLT).

I keep asking the God of our Loud Jesus Christ, the glorious Father, may give you the Spirit of wisdom and revelation, so that you may know Him better (Ephesians 1:17).

And lead us not into temptation, but deliver us from evil: For thine is the kingdom forever and ever (Mathew 6:13).

# Defeat the Enemies

And we praise God Most High, who has helped you to defeat your enemies (Genesis 14:20 NCV).

You'll chase out your enemies and defeat them (Leviticus 26:7 MSG)

*When people are hurting you and abusing you God is not with them and they will be defeated! This is God's promise to you:*

The Lord is not with you (those abusing you), and your enemies will defeat you (Numbers 14:42 GNT, comment mine).

The Lord says to you, "Do you see that great army?  I, the Lord, will defeat that army for you today.  Then you will know that I am the Lord (1 Kings 20:13).

Don't be afraid.  The army that fights for us is larger than the army that fights for Aram (2 Kings 6:16).

*That army is God's angelic host of angels fighting for you. Though you don't see them, they are there fighting for you because of your prayers and declaring Scriptures over yourself and circumstances.*

But David said, "No, my brothers! Don't be selfish with what the LORD has given us. He has kept us safe and helped us defeat the enemy (1 Samuel 30:23 NLT).

I will know you are pleased with me if my enemy doesn't defeat me. (Psalm 41:11 CJB).

The people of Judah will be victorious like soldiers who trample their enemies in the mud of the streets. They will fight because the Lord is with them, and they will defeat even the enemy cavalry (Zechariah 10:5 GNT).

And they were not able to resist the wisdom and the spirit which He spoke (Acts 6:10).

Then you shall understand the fear of the Lord and find the knowledge of God (Proverbs 2:5).

Do not be afraid of bad news.  They are confident because they trust the Lord (Psalm 112:7).

But those who listen to Me will live in safety and comfort. They will have nothing to fear (Proverbs 1:33).

Don't be afraid! Don't run away!  Stand where you are and watch the Lord save you today… You will not have to do anything but stay calm.  The Lord will do the fighting for you (Exodus 14:13).

# Depression

You will not conquer me because I am more than a conqueror thru Christ Jesus (Romans 8:37 paraphrased).

Lord those who know Your name come to You for protection and when they come, You do not leave them without help (Psalms 9:10).

But the Lord has called you back to Him... But with all My love, I will bring you back to Me again… I will comfort you with kindness forever (Isaiah 54:7-8).

Come to Me all of you who are tired from the heavy burden you have been forced to carry.  I will give you rest (Matthew 11:28).

Hurry and answer me, Lord!  I have lost my courage.  Do not run away from me…. Show me Your faithful love this morning.  I trust in You.  Show me what I should do (Psalms 143:7-8).

Do not be afraid, just believe (Mark 5:36).

Do not worry, I am with you.  Do not be afraid, I am your God.  I will make you strong, I will help you.  I will support you with My right hand that brings victory (Isaiah 41:10).

I am the Lord your God, who holds your right hand.  And I tell you, do not be afraid!  I will help you (Isaiah 41:13).

…but if you thinking is controlled by the Spirit, there is life and peace (Romans 8:6).

We capture every thought and make it give up and obey Christ (2 Corinthians 10:5).

I will give peace to those who are near and to those who are far away.  I will heal them.   The Lord Himself said this (Isaiah 7:19).

And they will shout for joy.  Their faces will shine with happiness about all the good things the Lord gives them.  They will be like a garden that has plenty of water.  I will change their sadness into happiness.  I will comfort My people, making them happy instead of sad (Jeremiah 31:12-14).

The Lord your God is with you.  He is like a powerful soldier, He will save you.  He will show you how much He loves you and how happy He is with you.  He will laugh and be happy about you like people at a party (Zephaniah 3:17-18).

# Emotional Abuse

To you, O Lord I lift up my soul. I trust in you, my God.  Do not let me disgraced, or let my enemies rejoice in my defeat. No one who trusts in You will ever be disgraced, but disgrace comes to those who try to deceive others (Psalm 25:1-3).

Turn to me and have mercy on me, for I am alone and in deep distress.  My problems go from bad to worse. Oh, save me from them all!  Do not let me be disgraced, for I trust in You. May integrity and honesty protect me, for I put my hope in You (Psalm 25:16-21).

The Lord will give strength to His people; the Lord will bless His people with peace (Psalm 29:11).

# Fear

The Lord says to you: Don't be afraid or worry about this large army, because the battle is not your battle.  It is God's battle (2 Chronicles 20:15b)!

You will not have to fight this battle.  Just stand there and watch the Lord save you… don't be afraid.  Don't worry, the Lord is with you.  So go out to stand against the people tomorrow (2 Chronicles 20:17).

God said Abraham, do not be afraid, I will defend you and give you a great reward (Genesis 15:2 ERV).

Do not be afraid, I am with you I will bless you.  I will make your family great (Genesis 26:24).

I am with you, and I will keep you wherever you go (Genesis 28:15).

Do not be afraid! Do not run away, stand where you are and watch the Lord save you today.  You will never see these

Egyptians again.  You will not have to do anything but stay calm.  The Lord will do the fighting for you (Exodus 14:13-14).

The Lord saved the Israelites every time there was trouble (Exodus 18:8).

When you fight against your enemies I will send my great power before you I will help you defeat all your enemies.  The people who are against you will become confused in battle and run away.  I will send a hornet in front of you he will force your enemies to leave (Exodus 23:27).

Do not be upset or afraid of those people.  The Lord your God is in front, leading you He will fight for you just as He did in Egypt (Deuteronomy 1:29-30).

# Financial Abuse

You will count your property and find nothing missing (Job 5:24).

David got back everything the Amalekites had taken, including his two wives. Nothing was missing. They found all the children and old people, all their sons and daughters and daughters and all their valuables (1 Samuel 30:18).

Let the Lord be the judge. Let Him decide between you and me. He will support me and show that I am right. He will save me from you (1 Samuel 24:15).

The Lord pays every man for what he does – He rewards him if he does right, and he punishes him if he does wrong (1 Samuel 26:23).

Then the king chose an officer to help her. The king said, "give to the woman all that belongs to her. And giver her all the harvest of her land from the day she left the country until now (2 Kings 8:6)."

And they said that an evil man suffers all his life.  A cruel man suffers all his numbered years.  Every noise scares him.  His enemy will attack him when he thinks he is safe.  An evil man has no hope of escaping the darkness.  There is a sword somewhere waiting to kill him.  He wanders from place to place looking for food.  But he knows a dark is coming, which he brought on himself.  He lives in fear, with warring and suffering threatening him like a king ready to attack.  That is because that evil man shook his fist at God, refusing to obey.  He dared to attack God All-Powerful… (Job 15:20-25).

"Here is what God has planned for those who are evil.  This is what cruel people will get from God All-Powerful… Evil people collect silver as easily as dirt.  They may have so many clothes that they are piled up like clay.  But their piles of clothes will be worn by those who have lived right.  All that silver will be given to those who have done no wrong.  Evil people might build houses, but they will not last long.  They will be like a spider's web or a guard's ten.  They might be rich when they go to bed, but when they open their eyes, all their riches will be gone.  Terrible fears will come over them like a flood, like a storm in the night that blows everything away.  The east wind will carry them away, and they will be gone.  The storm will sweep them out of their homes.  They may try to run away from the power of the storm, but it will come down on them without mercy… (Job 27:13-22).

# For I Am the Lord Who Heals You

For I, Jehovah, am healing thee (Exodus 15:26b YLT).

For I am the Lord, the one who heals you (Exodus 15:26b GNT).

I will keep you healthy... and I will give you long, full lives (Exodus 23:25 NLT).

And the Lord will protect you from all sickness (Deuteronomy 7:15 NLT).

The Lord your God will cleanse your heart and the hearts of all your descendants so that you will love Him with all your heart and soul and so you may live (Deuteronomy 30:6 NLT).

I have set before you today life and death... so choose life so that you may live (Deuteronomy 30:19 NASB)!

Do not be afraid, for I have ransomed you.  I have called you by name; you are Mine.  When you go through deep waters and great trouble, I will be with you.  When you go through rivers of difficulty, you will not drown!  When you walk through the fire of oppression, you will not be burned up; the flames will not consume you.  For I am the Lord your God, the Holy One of Israel, your Savior (Isaiah 43:1-3 NLT).

I have paid the price to set you free (Isaiah 44:22b NASB).

I will go before you and make the rough places smooth (Isaiah 45:2 NASB).

I created you and have cared for you since before you were born.  I will be your God throughout your lifetime – until your hair is white with age.  I made you, and I will care for you.  I will carry you along the way and save you (Isaiah 46:3-4).

I, even I, am He who comforts you (Isaiah 51:12 NASB).

For I know the plans I have for you declares the Lord, plans for good and not disaster, to give you a future and a hope (Jeremiah 29:11 NLT).

I know what I'm doing. I have it all planned out - plans to take care of you, not abandon you, plans to give you the future you hope for (Jeremiah 29:11 The Message).

Nothing is too difficult for Me (Jeremiah 32:17b GNT)!

For I am with you, declares the Lord, to save you (Jeremiah 30:11 NASB).

For I will restore you to health and I will heal you, declares the Lord (Jeremiah 30:17 NASB).

I will give you back your health and heal your wounds says the Lord (Jeremiah 30:17 NLT).

For I have given rest to the weary and joy to the sorrowing (Jeremiah 31:25 NLT).

For I will bring it to health and healing, and I will heal them; and I will reveal to them an abundance of peace and truth (Jeremiah 33:6 NASB)

Behold, I will apply a healing dressing to it and cure, and I will heal them, and will reveal unto them an abundance of peace and truth (Jeremiah 33:6 The Darby Translation).

# For Those Guilty of Abuse

And the Lord will by no means leave the guilty unpunished (Nahum 1:3 NASB).

The Lord Almighty says, "The day of judgment is coming, burning like a furnace.  The arrogant and the wicked will be burned up like straw on that day. The will be consumed like a tree – roots and all.   But for you who fear My name, the Sun of Righteousness will rise with healing with joy like calves let out to pasture. On the day when I act, you will tread upon the wicked as if they were dust under your feet," says the Lord Almighty (Malachi 4:1-3 NLT).

Arise, O Lord, in anger! Stand up against the fury of my enemies! Wake up, my God and bring justice! Gather the nations before you, sit on Your throne high above them, for I am innocent, O Most High! End the wickedness of the ungodly, but help all those who obey you. For you look deep within the mind and heart, O righteous God (Psalm 7:6-9 NLT).

God is my shield, saving those whose hearts are true and right. God is a judge who is perfectly fair. He is angry with the wicked every day. If a person does not repent, God will sharpen His sword; He will bend and string His bow. He will prepare His deadly weapons and ignite His flaming arrows (Psalm 7:10-13 NLT).

The wicked conceive evil; they are pregnant with trouble and give birth to lies. They dig a pit to trap other than fall into it themselves. They make trouble, but it backfires on them. They plan violence for others, but it befalls on their own heads (Psalm 7:6-16).

Do not rob the poor because they are poor or exploit the needy in court. For the Lord is their defender. He will injure anyone who injures them (Proverbs 22:22-23).

He does not forget the cry of the afflicted (Psalm 9:12).

They will be held guilty; they whose strength is their God (Habakkuk 1:11).

And He (God) said, "What have you done? The voice of your brother's blood is crying to Me from the ground (Genesis 4:10)."

*God is so sensitive to us and what is happening that the physical abuse done to us He feels.  When our blood cries out, He hears it!  He sees all!*

The Lord examines both the righteous and the wicked.  He hates everyone who loves violence.  He rains down blazing coals on the wicked, punishing them with burning sulfur and scorching winds.  For the Lord is righteous, and He loves justice. Those who do what is right will see His face (Psalm 11:5-7).

# Give God a Chance

Give the Lord a chance to show you how good He is.  Great blessings belong to those who depend on Him (Psalm 34:8)!

He is there to help even before the sunrise (Psalm 46:5).

When morning comes, the good people will enjoy victory (Psalm 49:14b).

Trust in the Lord – He is their help and shield (Psalm 115:9).

Trust in the Lord at all times, O people; pour out your hearts before Him.  God is our refuge.  Selah (Psalm 62:8).

# God Cares for Me

…You are the God who sees me (EL ROI) I see that even in this place God sees me and cares for me (Genesis 16:13).

God is with you in everything you do (Genesis 21:22).

"The Lord provides" (Yahweh Yireh)… He will give us what we need (Genesis 22:14).

Turn to the Lord for help in everything you do, and you will be successful (Proverbs 16:3).

Trust in the Lord completely, and do not depend on your own knowledge.  With every step you take, think about what He wants, and He will help you go the right way.  Do not trust in your own wisdom, but fear and respect the Lord and stay away from evil.  If you do this, it will be like a refreshing drink and medicine for your body (Proverbs 3:5).

People will make weapons to fight against you, but their weapons will not defeat you.  Some people will say things against you.  But anyone who speaks against you will be proved wrong.  The Lord says, "That is what my servants get!"  They get good things that come from Me (Isaiah 54:17).

# God Declares Me Innocent

The Lord rewarded me for doing right; He compensated me because of my innocence (Psalm 18:16-20).

Declare me innocent for You see those who do right (Psalm 17:2).

Declare me innocent O God defend me against these ungodly people (Psalm 43:1).

Declare me innocent O Lord!  For I have walked with integrity; I have trusted in the Lord without wavering.  Test me, O Lord, and try me; examine my heart and mind (Psalm 26:1)

# God Has Not Forgotten Me

It may seem that those who are poor and needy have been forgotten, but God will not forget them.  He will not leave them without hope (Psalms 9:18).

I always remember that the Lord is with me.  He is here, close by my side so nothing can defeat me.

He is there to help even before sunrise (Psalms 46:5).

The Lord provides for those He loves, even while they are sleeping (Psalms 127:26).

# God is My Protector and Shield

I love Thee, O'Lord, my strength. The Lord is my rock and my fortress and my deliverer. My God, my rock, in whom I take refuge; My shield and the horn of my salvation, my stronghold. I call upon the Lord, who is worthy to be praised. And I am saved from my enemies (Psalm 18:1-3).

My shield is God Most High, who saves the upright in heart (Psalm 7:10).

Put an end to the evil of the wicked, but establish the righteous, O Righteous God who searches hearts and minds (Psalm 7:10).

# God's Love for You

You are precious to me, I have given you a special place of honor.  I love you (Isaiah 43:4)

I have chosen you (Haggai 2:23).

If we are God's children, we will get the blessings God has for His people (Romans 8:17).

Can anything separate us from Christ's love?  Can any trouble or problems or persecution separate us from His love?  …but in all these troubles we have complete victory through God, who has shown His love for us.  Yes, I am sure that nothing can separate us from God's love – not death, life, angels, or ruling spirits.  I am sure that nothing now, nothing in the future, no powers, nothing above us or nothing below us – nothing in the whole created world – will ever be able to separate us from the love of God has shown us in Christ Jesus our Lord (Romans 8:35-39).

For God so loved the world that He gave His only Son, so that everyone who believes in Him will not perish but have eternal life (John 3:16 NLT).

For the Lord delights in you and will claim you as His own (Isaiah 62:4b NLT).

Long ago the Lord has said, "I have loved you, my people, with an everlasting love.  With unfailing love I have drawn you to myself… You again will be happy and dance merrily with tambourines (Jeremiah 31:3 NLT).

We pray that the Lord Jesus Christ Himself and God our Father will comfort you and strengthen you in every good thing you do and say.  God loved us and gave us through grace a wonderful hope and comfort that has no end (2 Thessalonians 2:16-17 ERV).

The Lord your God is with you and how happy He is with you.  He will laugh and be happy about you, like people at a party (Zephaniah 3:17 ERV).

I will show them My love without limits (Hosea 14:4b).

He loves those who try to do good (Proverbs 15:9).

But God so rich in His mercy, and He loved us so very much, that even while we were dead because of our own sins, He gave us life when He raised Christ from the dead. (It is only by God's special favor that you have been saved!) For He raised us from the dead along with Christ, and we are seated with Him in the heavenly realms—all because we are one with Christ Jesus. And so God can always point to us as examples of the incredible wealth of His favor and kindness toward us, as shown in all He has done for us through Christ Jesus (Ephesian 2:4-7 NLT).

God saved you by His special favor when you believed. And you can't take credit for this; it is a gift from God. Salvation is not a reward for the good things we have done, so none of us can boast about it. For we are God's masterpiece. He has created us anew in Christ Jesus, so that we can do the good things He planned for us so long ago (Ephesians 2:8 NLT).

God showed how much He loved us by sending His only Son into the world so that we might have eternal life through Him. This is real love. It is not that we loved God, but that He loved us and sent His Son as a sacrifice to take away our sins (1 John 4:9-10 NLT).

And I am convinced that nothing can ever separate us from His love. Death can't, and life can't. The angels can't and the demons can't. Our fears for today; our worries about tomorrow, and even the powers of heal can't keep God's love away. Whether we are high above the sky or in the deepest ocean, nothing in all creation will ever be able to separate us from the love of God that is reveals in Christ Jesus our Lord (Romans 8:38-39 NLT).

None of this fazes us because Jesus loves us. I am absolutely convinced that nothing—nothing living or dead, angelic or demonic, today or tomorrow, high or low, thinkable or unthinkable—absolutely nothing can get between us and God's love because of the way that Jesus our Master has embraced us (Romans 8:38-39 Message).

The Father Himself loves you dearly because you love Me (Jesus) and believe that I came from God (John 16:27).

I will be in them, and You will be in Me. So they will be completely one. Then the world will know that You sent Me and that You loved them just as You loved Me (John 17:23 ERV).

We know this because God has poured out His love to fill our hearts through the Holy Spirit He gave us (Romans 5:5).

Can anything separate us from Christ's love? Can trouble or problems or persecution separate us from His love? If we have no food or clothing or face danger or even death, will that separate us from His love? As the Scriptures says, "for we are in danger of death all the time. People think we are worth no more that sheep to be killed." But in all these troubles we have complete victory through God, who has shown his love for us.  Yes, I am sure that nothing can separate us from God's love—not death, life, angels, or ruling spirits.  I am sure that nothing now, nothing in the future, no powers, nothing above us or nothing below us—nothing in the whole created world—will ever be able to separate us in Christ Jesus our Lord (Romans 8:35-38 ERV).

# God Sends an Army to Defeat My Armies

Elisha said, "Don't be afraid.  The army that fights for us is larger than the army that fights for Aram.   Then Elisha prayed and said, Lord, I ask you, open my servant's eyes so that he can see."  The Lord opened the eyes of the young man, and the servant saw the mountain was full of horses and chariots of fire.   They were all around Elisha (2 Kings6:16-17 ERV).

I, the Lord, am a god of the mountains and not a god of the valleys.  So I will let you defeat this great army.  Then all you will know I AM the Lord, wherever you are (1 Kings 20:28)!

Do you see the great army?  I, the Lord, will defeat that army for you today.  Then you will know that I am the Lord (1 Kings 20:13).

Every time Israel went out to battle, the Lord fought against them, causing them to be defeated, just as He had warned. And the people were in great distress (Judges 2:15).

We are troubled on every side, but not crushed; perplexed but not in despair (2 Corinthians 4:8).

But those who wait on the Lord will renew their strength; they will mount up with wings like eagles; they will run and not grow weary; they will walk and not faint (Isaiah 40:31).

In every way we're troubled, but we aren't crushed by our troubles.  We're frustrated but we don't give up (2 Corinthians 4:8).

# God Will Defeat the Enemies Sent Against Us

Don't be afraid!  Don't run away!  Stand where you are and watch the Lord save you today.  You will never see these Egyptians again.  You will not have to do anything but stay calm.  The Lord will do the fighting for you.

The Lord will make you strong and you will defeat your enemies (paraphrased Deuteronomy 33:7b).

The Lord saved Israelites every time there was trouble (Exodus 18:8b).

God who has always helped me during times of trouble, He has been with me wherever I have gone (Genesis 35:3b).

I am with you, and I will protect you wherever you go (Genesis 28:15).

I will defend you and give you a great reward (Genesis 15:1).

Do not be afraid, for I have ransomed you. I have called you by name; you are Mine. When you go through deep waters and great trouble, I will be with you. When you go through rivers of difficulty, you will not drown! When you walk through the fire of oppression, you will not be burned up; the flames will not consume you. For I am the Lord your God, the Holy One of Israel, your Savior (Isaiah 43:1-3 NLT).

I have paid the price to set you free (Isaiah 44:22b NASB).

I will go before you and make the rough places smooth (Isaiah 45:2 NASB).

I created you and have cared for you since before you were born. I will be your God throughout your lifetime – until your hair is white with age. I made you, and I will care for you. I will carry you along the way and save you (Isaiah 46:3-4).

I, even I, am He who comforts you (Isaiah 51:12 NASB).

For I know the plans I have for you declares the Lord, plans for good and not disaster, to give you a future and a hope (Jeremiah 29:11 NLT).

I know what I'm doing. I have it all planned out - plans to take care of you, not abandon you, plans to give you the future you hope for (Jeremiah 29:11 The Message).

Nothing is too hard for Me (Jeremiah 32:17b NLT)!

Nothing is too difficult for Me (Jeremiah 32:17b GNT)!

For I am with you, declares the Lord, to save you (Jeremiah 30:11 NASB).

God will fight for you just as He promised (Joshua 23:19).

The Lord has driven out great and powerful nations before you, and to this day no one can stand against you.  One of you can put a thousand to flight, because the Lord your God fights for you, just as He promised.  Therefore, watch yourselves carefully, that you love the Lord your God... (Joshua 23:9-11).

# God Will Fight for Us

God will fight for us (Nehemiah 4:20b)!

Lord, when you bless good people, you surround them with your life, like a large shield that protects them (Psalm 5:12).

I love Thee, O'Lord, my strength. The Lord is my rock and my fortress and my deliverer. My God, my rock, in whom I take refuge; My shield and the horn of my salvation, my stronghold. I call upon the Lord, who is worthy to be praised. And I am saved from my enemies (Psalm 18:1-3).

He reached down from heaven and rescued me; He drew me out of deep waters. He delivered me from my powerful enemies, from those who hated me and were too strong for me. They attacked me at a moment when I was weakest, but the Lord upheld me. He led me to a place of safety; He rescued me because He delights in me.

You will feel safe because there is hope.  God will protect you and give you rest.  You will lie down without fear of anyone (Job: 11:18-19).

Lord, those who know your name come to you for protection. And when they come, you do not leave them without help.

But those who go to Him for protection will be blessed (Psalm 2:12b).

But you, Lord, protect me.  You bring honor; you give me hope (Psalm 3:1).

# Habakkuk's Vision

1 The divine revelation that the prophet Habakkuk saw.

## Habakkuk's Question

2 How long, O **Yahweh**, am I to cry for help,
  but you will not listen?
  I cry out to you, "There's violence!"
  yet you will not come to the rescue.
3 Why do you make me see wrongdoing?
  And why do you watch wickedness?
  Destruction and violence are in front of me.
  Quarrels and disputes arise.
4 That is why your teaching is numbed,
  and justice is never carried out.
    Wicked people surround righteous people
      so that when justice is carried out, it's perverted.

## The LORD's Answer

5 Look among the nations and watch.
  Be amazed and astonished.
  I am going to do something in your days that you would

not believe even if it were reported to you.

⁶ I am going to send the Babylonians,

  that fierce and reckless nation.

    They will march throughout the earth

    to take possession of lands that don't belong to them.

⁷ They will be terrifying and fearsome.

    They will carry out their own kind of justice and honor.

⁸ Their horses will be faster than leopards

    and quicker than wolves in the evening.

    Their riders will gallop along proudly.

    Their riders will come from far away.

    They will fly like an eagle that swoops down for its prey.

⁹ They will all come for violence.

    Every face will be directed forward.

    They will gather prisoners like sand.

¹⁰ They will make fun of kings and treat rulers as a joke.

    They will laugh at every fortified city

    and build a dirt ramp to capture it.

¹¹ They will move quickly and pass through like the wind.

    So they will be guilty,

        because their own strength is their god.

# Healing Scriptures for Abuse

The Lord has redeemed my life from all distress (2 Samuel 4:9).

I cry out to the Lord and He heals me (Psalm 30:2).

The Lord forgives all my sins and heals all my diseases (Psalm 103:3).

He sends His Word and heals me and rescues me from the pit and destruction (Psalm 107:20).

He heals my broken heart and binds up my wounds, curing my pains and sorrows (Psalm 147:3).

The Lord has declared that He will restore me to health and heal my wounds (Jeremiah 30:17).

For you Lord have been a defense for the helpless, a defense for the needy in his distress, a refuge from the storm, a shade from the heat (Isaiah 25:4).

And the Lord God will wipe tears away from all faces, and He will remove the reproach of His people from all the earth; for the Lord has spoken (Isaiah 25:8).

You will guard me and keep me in perfect peace because my mind is stayed on You (Isaiah 26:3).

I will weep no longer. He will surely be gracious to me and at the sound of my cry, when He hears it He will answer me (Isaiah 30:19).

And my ears will hear a word behind me saying, "This is the way, walk in it," whenever you turn to the right or to the left (Isaiah 30:21).

I hear the Lord, He speaks to me and I know His voice.

Everlasting joy is upon my head. I will find gladness and joy, and sorrow and sighing will flee away (Isaiah 35:10).

You are My servant, I have chosen you.  Do not fear, for I am with you; do not anxiously look about you, for I am your God.  I will strengthen you, surely I will help you, surely I will uphold you with My righteous right hand (Isaiah 41:9-10).

Behold, I will do something new, now it will spring forth; will you not be aware of it?  I will even make a road way in the wilderness and rivers in the desert (Isaiah 43:19).

I will go before you and make the rough places smooth… I will give you the treasures of darkness, and hidden wealth of secret places, in order that you may know that it is I, the Lord, the God of Israel who calls you by name… My chosen one, I have also called you by your name; I have given you a title of honor (Isaiah 45:2-4).

I, even I, am He who comforts you (Isaiah 51:12).

For the Lord will go ahead of me and the God of Israel will protect me from behind (Isaiah 52:12).

I have been given a garland of beauty instead of ashes, and I have been given the oil of joy instead of mourning, and the garment of expressive praise instead of a heavy, burdened, and failing spirit (Isaiah 61:7).

But now, O Lord, You are my Father, and I am the clay, and you are the Potter; and I am the work of Your hand (Isaiah 64:8).

# He Will Calm All Your Fears

But I called on Your Name, Lord, from deep within the well, and you heard me!  You listened to my pleading; you heard my weeping!  Yes, You came at my despairing cry and told me, "Do not fear."  Lord, you are my Lawyer!  Plead my case! For you have redeemed my life.  You have seen the wrong they have done to me, Lord.  Be my judge, and prove me right.  You have seen the plots my enemies have laid against me.  Lord you have heard the vial names they call me.  You know all about the plans they have made – the plots against me all day long.  Look at them!  In all their activities, they constantly mock me with their songs.  Pay them back, Lord, for all the evil they have done.  Give them hard and stubborn hearts and then let your curse fall upon them!  Case them in your anger, destroying them from beneath the Lord's heavens." (Lamentations 3:55-66)

Fear not, the Lord is a jealous God, filled with vengeance and wrath.  He takes revenge on all who oppose Him and furiously destroys His enemies.  The Lord is slow to get angry, but His power is great, and He never lets the guilty go unpunished.  He displays His power in the whirlwind and the storm.  The billowing clouds are the dust beneath His feet.  At His command the oceans and rivers dry up, the lush pastures of Bashan and Carmel fade, and the green forests of Lebanon wilt.  In His presence the mountains quake, and the hills melt away; the earth trembles and its people are destroyed…The Lord is good.  When trouble comes, He is a strong refuge.  And He knows everyone who trust I Him.  But He sweeps away His enemies in an overwhelming flood.  He pursues His foes into the darkness of night (Nahum 1:1-8).

And the Lord himself, the King of Israel, will live among you!  At last your troubles will be over, and you will fear disaster no more.  On that day the announcement will be "Cheer up!  Don't be afraid! For the Lord your God has arrived to live among you.  He is a mighty Savior.  He will rejoice over you with great gladness.  With His love, He will calm all your fears.  He will exult over you by singing a happy song (Zephaniah 3:15-17).

# Justice

Lord, get up and show your anger!  My enemy is angry, so stand and fight against him.  Get me the justice that You demand.  Gather the nations around You and take Your place and judge.  Lord, judge the people.  Lord, judge me.  Prove that I am right and that I am innocent (Psalm 7:8).

The Lord set up his throne to bring justice, and He will rule forever.  He judges everyone on earth fairly… Many people are suffering—crushed by the weight of their troubles.  But the Lord is a refuge for them, a safe place they can run to (Psalm 7:7-9).

Lord, you know the hopes of the helpless. Surely you will listen to their cries and comfort them. You will bring justice to the orphans and the oppressed, so people can no longer terrify them (Psalm 10:17-18).

The Lord hates these two things: punishing the innocent and letting the guilty go free (Proverbs 17:15).

Don't ever say, "I'll pay them back for what they did to me!" Wait for the Lord, He will make things right (Proverbs 20:22 ERV).

Therefore, the Lord longs to be gracious to you, and therefore He waits on high to have compassion one you.  For the Lord is a God of justice; How blessed are all those who long for Him (Isaiah 30:18).

The Lord is a jealous God.  The Lord punishes the guilty, and He is very angry.  The Lord punishes his enemies and stays angry with them (Nahum 1:2).

He pleads my case and executes justice for me. He will bring me out to the light and I will see His righteousness.  Then my enemy will see and shame will cover her who said to me, "Where is the Lord your God?" (Micah 7:9-10)

He (God) will not give up until He has made justice victorious (Matthew 12:20b).

He will make your innocence as clear as the dawn, and the justice of your cause will shine like the noonday sun (Psalm 37:6).

Give fair judgment to the poor and the orphans; uphold the rights of the oppressed and the destitute. Rescue the poor and helpless deliver them from the grasp of evil people (Psalm 82:3-4).

Because the Sovereign Lord helps me, I will not be dismayed. Therefore, I have set my face like a stone, determined to do His will. And I know that I will triumph. He who gives me justice is near… See, the Sovereign Lord is on my side (Isaiah 50:7-9).

He (the Lord) will take up my case and punish my enemies from all the evil they have done to me. The Lord will bring me out of my darkness into the light, and I will see His righteousness (Micah 7:9 NLT).

And the Lord will by no means leave the guilty unpunished (Nahum 1:3b).

When justice is done, it brings joy to the righteous but terror to evildoers (Proverbs 21:15).

Whoever says to the guilty, "You are innocent," will be cursed by peoples and denounced by nations.
But it will go well with those who convict the guilty, and rich blessing will come on them (Proverbs 24:24-25).

# Living in Safety

In peace I will both lie down and sleep, for Thou alone, O Lord, dost make me to dwell in safety (Psalm 4:8).

You will have your fill of food to eat and will dwell securely in your land.  And I will give you peace to the land and you will lie down with nothing to fear. I will rid the land of dangerous animals, and no sword will pass through your land (Leviticus 26:5b-6).

You are to keep My statues and carefully observe My judgements, so that you may dwell securely in the land (Leviticus 25:18).

God is our refuge and strength, a very present help in trouble (Psalm 46:1-7).

# Obedient to the Lord

He (Hezekiah) was very faithful to the Lord and did not stop following Him.  He kept the commands that the Lord had given to Moses.  The Lord was with Hezekiah, so he was successful in everything he did (2 Kings 18:6-7).


If you follow His teaching exactly, you will be successful in everything you do.  Always remember what is written in the book of the law.  Speak about it day and night.  Then you can be sure to obey what is written there.  If you do this, you will be wise and successful in everything you do. Remember, I commanded you to be strong and brave.  Don't be afraid, because the Lord your God will be with you wherever you go (Joshua 1:7b-9).

# Peace

I am giving you peace from all of your enemies (2 Samuel 7:11 b).

All the people were happy and the city was peaceful (2 Kings 11:20).

God gives me peace in my land, and I will be able to sleep without fear.  He will remove the wild animals from my land and protect me from my enemies… all my enemies will fall (Leviticus 26:6-8b NLT).

I will remain unharmed and peaceful (2 Samuel 17:3b NLT).

The Lord has granted me peace throughout the entire land and I live in peace and safety and have peace on all sides (1 Kings 4:24b, 25b).

 I will experience peace and rest; the Lord will give me peace with my enemies in all the surrounding lands and the Lord will give me peace and quietness (1 Chronicles 22:9).

I am His; therefore, He gives me strength and blesses me with peace (Psalm 29:11 NLT).

He rescues me and keeps me safe and delivers my soul in peace from the battle waged against me (Psalm 55:18 NLT/KJV).

I listen carefully to what God the Lord is saying, for He speaks peace to me, His faithful one (Psalm 85:8 NLT).

I do not forget His Laws; and my heart keeps His commandments; therefore, the length of days and long life and peace will be added to me (Proverbs 3:1-2 KJV).

Because my ways pleases the Lord, He makes my enemies live at peace with me (Proverbs 16:7 NLT).

My thoughts are fixed on the Lord and I trust Him; therefore, I will keep in perfect peace (Isaiah 26:3 NLT).

The Lord has granted me peace (Proverbs 26:12 NLT).

My righteousness will bring peace. Quietness and confidence will fill my land forever (Isaiah 32:17).

# Physical Abuse

This is what the Lord God said, "I washed you in water. I poured water over you and washed away the blood that was on you, and then I put oil on your skin. I gave you a nice dress and soft leather sandals, a linen headband, and a silk scarf. I also gave you some jewelry. I put bracelets on your arms and a necklace around your neck. I gave you a nose ring, earrings, and a beautiful crown to wear. You were beautiful in your gold and silver jewelry, and your linen, silk and embroidered material. You ate the best foods. You were very, very beautiful, and you became the queen! You became famous for your beauty, all because I made you so lovely!" This is what the Lord God said (Ezekiel 16:8-14 ERV).

Sing and be happy! Shout for Joy! Be happy and have fun! … The Lord is with you. You don't need to worry about anything bad happening. …Be strong, don't be afraid! The Lord your God is with you. He is like a powerful soldier. He will save you. He will show how much He loves you and how happy He is with you. He will laugh and be happy about you, like people at a party. I will take away your shame. I will make them stop hurting you. At that time, I will punish those who hurt you. I will save my hurt people and bring back those who were forced to leave. I will give them praise and honor everywhere, even in places they suffered shame. You will see me bring back all the blessings you once had. This is what the Lord said (Zephaniah 3:14-20 ERV).

Lord have mercy on me.  See how I suffer at the hands of those who hate me. Snatch me back from the jaws of death. Save me, so I can praise you publicly at Jerusalem's gates (Psalm 9:13-14).

He does not forget the cries of the afflicted (Psalm 9:12b NASB).

And the one who loves violence His soul hates.  Upon the wicked he will rain stares; fire and brimstone and burning wind will be the portion of their cup.  For the Lord is righteous; He loves righteousness; the upright will behold His face (Psalm 11:5-7).

The Lord hears His people when they call to Him for help. He rescues them from all their troubles.  The Lord is close to the brokenhearted; He rescues those who are crushed in spirit.  The righteous face many troubles, but the Lord rescues them from each and every one.  For the Lord protects them from harm – not one of their bones will be broken (Psalm 34:17-20)!

Come with great power, O God, and rescue me! Defend me with Your might. O God, listen to my prayer. Pay attention to my plea.  For strangers are attacking me; violent men are trying to kill me. They care nothing for God.  But God is my helper. The Lord is the one who keeps me alive! May my enemies' plans for evil be turned against them.  Do as you promised and put an end to them (Psalm 54:1-5).

# Prosperity

If they obey and serve Him, they shall spend their days in prosperity, and their years in pleasure (Job 36:11 KJV).

This book of the law shall not depart out of your mouth; but you shall meditate on it, day and night, so that you may be careful to do according to all that is written in it; for then you will make your way prosperous and then you will have success (Joshua 1:8 NASB).

Let the Lord be magnified, which hath pleasure in the prosperity of His servants (Psalm 35:27b KJV).

That I may cause those that love Me to inherit substance; and I will fill their treasures (Proverbs 8:21 KJV).

And I will give you treasures hidden in the darkness – secret riches (Isaiah 45:3 NLT).

I will go before you and make the rough places smooth.  I will shatter the doors of bronze and cut through their own bars.  And I will give you the treasure of darkness and hidden wealth of secret places in order that you may know that it is I, the Lord, the God of Israel, who calls you by name (Isaiah 45:2-3 NASB).

Enlarge the place of your tent, stretch out the curtains of your dwellings, spare not, lengthen your cords and strengthen your pegs.  For you will spread abroad to the right and to the left and your descendants will possess the nations (Isaiah 54:2-3 NASB).

Arise shine for your light has come and the glory of the Lord has risen upon you… Then you will see and be radiant and your heart will thrill and rejoice because the abundance of the sea will be turned to you.  The wealth of the nations will come to you, a multitude of camels will cover you… and all those from Sheba will come, they will bring gold and frankincense…  So that men may bring to you the wealth of nations… the glory of Lebanon will come to you, the juniper, the box tree, the cypress together… and the sons of those who have afflicted you will come bowing down to you (Isaiah 60 NASB [read all of it, it's very encouraging!]).

But you will be called priests of the Lord, you will be spoken about as ministers of our God.  You will eat the wealth of nations and in their riches, you will boast.  Instead of shame, you will have double portion in their land, everlasting joy is theirs (Isaiah 61:6-8 NASB).

And you will seek Me and find Me, when you search for Me with all your heart.  And I will be found by you, declares the Lord, and I will restore your fortunes (Jeremiah 29:13-14 NASB).

Restrain your voice from weeping and your eyes from tears for your work SHALL be rewarded (Isaiah 31:16 NASB).

There is hope for your future, declares the Lord (Isaiah 31:17 NASB).

… I am the Lord thy God which teaches thee to profit, which leadeth thee by the way that thou shall go (Isaiah 48:17b KJV).

For the Lord is a God of recompense, He will fully repay (Isaiah 51:56b NASB).

And I will put My Spirit within you and you will come to life and I will place you on your own land.  Then you will know that I the Lord have spoken and done it, declares the Lord (Ezekiel 37:14 NASB).

Take courage, declares the Lord and work, for I am with you, says the Lord of Hosts.  As for the promises which I made you when you came out of Egypt, My spirit is abiding in your midst, do not fear!  For thus says the Lord of Hosts, once more in a little while, I am going to shake the heaven and the earth, and the sea also and the dry land.  And I will shake all the nations and they will come with the wealth of all nations and I will fill this house with glory says the Lord of hosts.  The silver is Mine, and the gold is Mine, declares the Lord of Hosts.  The latter glory of this house will be greater than the former, says the Lord of Hosts, and in this place I shall give peace, declares the Lord of Hosts (Haggai 2:4-9 NASB).

From this day on, I will bless you (Haggai 2:19b NASB).

But you shall remember the Lord your God for it is He who has given you power to make wealth, that He may confirm His Covenant (Deuteronomy 8:18 NASB).

# Protection

Let the Lord be the judge.  Let Him decide between you and me.  He will support me and show that I am right.  He will save me from you (1 Samuel 24:15).

The Lord pays every man for what he does – He rewards him if he does right, and he punishes him if he does wrong (1 Samuel 26:23).

God made my family strong and secure.  He made an agreement with me forever.  God make sure this agreement was good and secure in every way.  So surely he will give me every victory.  He will give me everything I want (2 Samuel 23:5).

In the same way the Lord will show that my life is important to Him.  He will save me from every trouble (1 Samuel 26:24b).

David got back everything the Amalekites had taken, including his two wives. Nothing was missing. They found all the children and old people, all their sons and daughters and daughters and all their valuables (1 Samuel 30:18).

But now the Lord my god has given me peace along all the borders of my country.  I have no enemies, and my people are in no danger.

God will fight for us (Nehemiah 4:20b)!

Lord, when you bless good people, you surround them with your life, like a large shield that protects them (Psalm 5:12).

But those who go to Him for protection will be blessed (Psalm 2:12b).

But you, Lord, protect me.  You bring honor; you give me hope (Psalm 3:1).

Guard my life and rescue me; do not let me put to shame, for I take refuge in you (Psalm 25:20.

The Lord shall preserve you from all evil; He shall preserve your soul (Psalm 121:7).

The Lord says to you: Don't be afraid or worry about this large army, because the battle is not your battle.  It is God's battle (2 Chronicles 20:15b)!

You will not have to fight this battle.  Just stand there and watch the Lord save you… don't be afraid.  Don't worry, the Lord is with you.  So go out to stand against the people tomorrow (2 Chronicles20:17).

# Protection from the Enemy

The Lord's angels build a camp around His followers, and He protects them (Psalm 34:7).


Your laws can be trusted!  Protect me from cruel liars (Psalm 119:86).


All Your commandments are faithful; I am persecuted without cause – help me (Psalm 119:86)!


Let not my enemies gloat over me without cause, or those who hate me without reason maliciously wink their eye (Psalm 109:26).

# Protection from Abusers

You will feel safe because there is hope.  God will protect you and give you rest.  You will lie down without fear of anyone (Job: 11:18-19).

Lord, those who know your name come to you for protection. And when they come, you do not leave them without help.

God shall likewise destroy you (abusers) forever, He shall take you away (Psalm 52:5-7).

Protect me from the wicked people who attack me, from murderous enemies who surround me (Psalm 17:9).

You will feel safe because there is hope.  God will protect you and give you rest.  You will lie down without fear of anyone.  Job: 11:18-19

Lord, those who know your name come to you for protection. And when they come, you do not leave them without help.

**The reward of the wicked:**

Evil people might look for help, but they will not escape their troubles.  Their hope leads only to death (Job 11:20).

He (God) exposes even the darkest secrets (Job 12:22).

And they said that an evil man suffers all his life.  A cruel man suffers all his numbered years.  Every noise scares him. His enemy will attack him when he thinks he is safe.  An evil man has no hope of escaping the darkness.  There is a sword somewhere waiting to kill him.  He wanders from place to place looking for food.  But he knows a dark is coming, which he brought on himself.  He lives in fear, with worrying and suffering threatening him like a king ready to attack. That is because that evil man shook his fist at God, refusing to obey.  He dared to attack God All-Powerful… (Job 15:20-25).

Here is what God has planned for those who are evil.  This is what cruel people will get from God All-Powerful… Evil people collect silver as easily as dirt.  They may have so may clothes that they are piled up like clay.  But their piles of clothes will be worn by those who have lived right.  All that silver will be given to those who have done no wrong.  Evil people might build houses, but they will not last long.  They will be like a spider's web or a guard's ten.  They might be rich when they go to bed, but when they open their eyes, all their riches will be gone.  Terrible fears will come over them like a flood, like a storm in the night that blows everything away.  The east wind will carry them away, and they will be gone.  The storm will sweep them out of their homes.  They may try to run away from the power of the storm, but it will come down on them without mercy… (Job 27:13-22)

# Protection & Security

Let the Lord be the judge.  Let Him decide between you and me.  He will support me and show that I am right.  He will save me from you (1 Samuel 24:15).

The Lord pays every man for what he does – He rewards him if he does right, and he punishes him if he does wrong (1 Samuel 26:23).

God made my family strong and secure.  He made an agreement with me forever.  God make sure this agreement was good and secure in every way.  So surely, He will give me every victory.  He will give me everything I want (2 Samuel 23:5).

In the same way the Lord will show that my life is important to Him.  He will save me from every trouble (1 Samuel 26:24b).

But now the Lord my God has given me peace along all the borders of my country.  I have no enemies, and my people are in no danger (1 Kings 5:4).

Keep me as the apple of Your eye; hide me in the shadow of Your wings, from the wicked who assail me, from my mortal enemies who surround me.  They have closed their callous hearts; their mouths speak with arrogance… (Psalm 17:8-10).

But now the Lord has given me rest on every side and there is no adversary or crisis (1 Kings 5:4).

But those who go to Him for protection will be blessed.  Psalm (2:12b).

But you, Lord, protect me.  You bring honor; you give me hope (Psalm 3:1)

God, you showed that I was innocent.  You gave me relief from all my troubles (Psalm 4:1).

You destroy those who tells lies.  Lord, you hate those who make secret plans to hurt others (Psalm 5:6)

God helps people who want to do right, so He will protect me. God is a good judge. He always condemns evil. (Psalm 7:10-11)

Lord, get up and show your anger! My enemy is angry, demand. Gather the nations around you and take your place and judge. Lord, judge the people. Lord, judge me. Prove that I am right and that I am innocent (Psalm 7:8)

The Lord set up his throne to bring justice, and he will rule forever. He judges everyone on earth fairly… Many people are suffering—crushed by the weight of their troubles. But the Lord is a refuge for them, a safe place they can run to (Psalm 7:7-9).

# Prayer/Scripture Over My House

I declare: Peace and prosperity to me, my family and everything I own (1Samuel 25:6)!

The Lord has granted me peace throughout the entire land and I live in peace and safety and have peace on all sides (1 Kings 4:24b, 25b).

My righteousness will bring peace. Quietness and confidence will fill my land forever (Isaiah 32:17).

I am His, therefore I will live in peaceable habitations, and in sure dwellings, and in quite resting places (Isaiah 32:18 KJV).

I will live in safety, quietly at home and I will be at rest (Isaiah 32:18 NLT).

Lord according to your Word I declare over myself: The Lord Almighty says: In just a little while I will again shake the heavens and the earth.  I will shake the oceans and the dry land, too.   I will shake the nations and the treasures of all the nations will come to this Temple.  I will fill this place with glory, says the Lord Almighty.  The silver is mine, and the gold is mine, says the Lord Almighty.  The future glory of this Temple will be greater than its past glory, says the Lord Almighty.  And in this place I will bring peace.  I the Lord have spoken (Haggai 2:6-9 NLT)!

God gives me peace in my land, and I will be able to sleep without fear.  He will remove the wild animals from my land and protect me from my enemies… all my enemies will fall (Leviticus 26:6,8b NLT).

I declare abounding peace and prosperity on me and my house (Daniel 4:1b).

And my house and my kingdom shall endure before God forever; your throne shall be established forever (2 Samuel 7:17).

Thus, the ark of the Lord remains in my house and the Lord blessed me and my entire household. The Lord has blessed my house and all that belongs to me on account of the ark of God.  The presence of God is present on this house and the blessings of God shines forth for all to see and He blesses those who see Him (2 Samuel 6:11-12 paraphrased).

The glory of the Lord fills this house (1 Kings 8: 10-11).

That Thine eyes may be opened towards this house day and night and toward the place of which Thou has said, "My name shall be there, to listen to the prayer which Thy servant shall pray towards this place (1 Kings 8:29)."

And listen to the supplication of Thy servant and when I pray towards this place; hear Thou in heaven Thy dwelling place; hear and forgive (1 Kings 8:30).

Hear Thou in heaven and forgive the sin of Thy servants and of Thy people, indeed, teach them the good way in which they should walk.  And send rain on Thy land which Thou hast given Thy people for an inheritance (1 Kings 8:36).

And the Lord said to me, "I have heard your prayer and your supplication, which you have made before Me; I have consecrated this house which you have built by putting My name there forever, and my eyes and My heart will be there perpetually (1: Kings 9:3).

And now, O Lord God, Thou art God, and Thy words are truth, and Thou hast promised this good thing to Thy servant. Now therefore, may it please Thee to bless the house of Thy servant, that it may continue forever before Thee, For Thou, O Lord God, hast spoken; and with Thy blessing may the house of Thy servant be blessed forever (2 Samuel 7: 28-29).

The Spirit of the Lord spoke to me, and His Word was on my tongue. The God of Israel said, The Rock of Israel spoke to me, He who rules over men righteously, who rules in the fear of God, is as the light of the morning when the sun rises, A morning without clouds, When the tender grass springs out of the earth, through sunshine after rain, truly is not my house so with God? For He has made an everlasting covenant with me, ordered in all things and secured, for all my salvation and all my desire, will He not indeed make it grow (2 Samuel 23:2-5)?

Behold, He who keeps Israel will neither slumber nor sleep. The Lord is your keeper; the Lord is your shade on your right hand. The sun will not smite you by day, nor the moon by night. The Lord will protect you from all evil; He will keep you soul. The Lord will guard your going out and your coming in from this time forth and forever (Psalm 121:4-8).

May peace be within your walls, and prosperity within your palaces. For the sake of my brothers and my friends, I will now say may peace be within you (Psalm 122: 7-9).

Our help is in the name of the Lord, who made heaven and earth (Psalm 124:8).

For the Lord has chosen Zion; He has desired it for His habitation.  This is My resting place forever; Here I will dwell, for I have desired it.  I will abundantly bless her provision; I will satisfy her needy with bread (Psalm 132:13-15).

Arise shine; for your light has come, and the glory of the Lord has risen upon you…. the Lord will rise upon you (Isaiah 60:1-2).

Instead of your shame you will have a double portion, and instead of humiliation they will shout for joy over their portion.  Therefore, they will possess double portion in their land.  Everlasting joy will be theirs.  For I the Lord love justice, I hate robbery in the burnt offering; I will faithfully give them their recompense, and I will make an everlasting covenant with them. Then their offspring will be known among the nations and their descendants in the midst of people. All who see them will recognize them because they are the offspring whom the Lord has blessed (Isaiah 61:7-11).

# Rescue Me from My Abuser

He reached down from heaven and rescued me; He drew me out of deep waters. He delivered me from my powerful enemies, from those who hated me and were too strong for me.  They attacked me at a moment when I was weakest, but the Lord upheld me.  He led me to a place of safety; He rescued me because He delights in me.

Their violence has grown into a rod to punish their wickedness.  None of them will remain: none of their multitude, none of their wealth, and nothing of value (Ezekiel 7:11).

And I will set My jealous rage against you, and they will deal with you in fury (Ezekiel 23:25a).

# Restoration of All That Belongs to You

David got back everything the Amalekites had taken, including his two wives.  Nothing was missing.  They found all the children and old people, all their sons and daughters and daughters and all their valuables (1 Samuel 30:18).

Then the king chose an officer to help her.  The king said, "give to the woman all that belongs to her.  And giver her all the harvest of her land from the day she left the country until now (2 Kings 8:6)."

I will before you and make the rough place smooth.  I will shelter the doors of bronze and cut thin their own bars.  I will give you the treasure of darkness and hidden wealth of secret places in order that you may know that it is I, the Lord, the God of Israel who calls you by your name (Isaiah 45:2-3).

Enlarge the place of you tent, stretch out the curtains of your dwellings, spare not. Lengthen your cords and strengthen you pegs for you will spread aboard to the right and to the left and your descendants will possess the nations (Isaiah 54:2-3 NASB).

Arise, and shine; for your light has come, and the glory of the Lord has risen upon you... Then you will see and be radiant and your heart will thrill and rejoice; because the abundance of the sea will turn to you. The wealth of the nations will come to you. A multitude of camels will cover you…. All those from Sheba will come. They will bring gold and frankincense… So that men may bring to you the wealth of the nations…. the glory of Lebanon will come to you the juniper, the box tree, and the cypress together, to beautify the place of My sanctuary; and I shall make the place of My feet glorious. And the sons of those who afflicted you will come bowing to you, and all those who despised you will bow themselves at the sole of your feet; and they will call you the city of the Lord, the Zion of the Holy One of Israel (Isaiah 60).

…but you will be called priests of the Lord, you will be spoken of as ministers of our God. You will eat the wealth of nations, and in their riches, you will boast. Instead of your shame you will have a double portion, and instead of humiliation they will shout for joy over their portion. Therefore, they will possess a double portion in their land, everlasting joy will be theirs (Isaiah 61:6-8).

If you seek Me and find Me, when you search for Me with all your heart.  And I will be found by you, declares the Lord, and I will restore your fortunes… (Jeremiah 29:13-14).

Restrain your voice from weeping and your eyes from tears; for your work shall be rewarded (Jeremiah 31:16).

For the Lord is a God of recompense.  He will fully repay (Jeremiah 51:56b NASB).

And I will put My Spirit with in you and you will come to life and I will place you on your own land.  Then you will know that I, the Lord, have spoken and done it, declares the Lord (Ezekiel 37:14).

And I will give you treasures hidden in the darkness, secret riches (Isaiah 45:3 LT).

I would have given you much more… (2 Samuel 12:7-17).

…take courage, declares the Lord, and work; for I am with you, says the Lord of host.  As for the promise which I made you when you came out of Egypt, My Spirit is abiding in your midst; do not fear!  For thus says the Lord of host, once more in a little while, I am going to shake the heavens and the earth, the sea also and the dry land.  And I will shake all the nations; and they will come with the wealth of all nations; and I will fill this house with glory, says the Lord of hosts.  The silver is Mine, and the gold is Mine, declares the Lord of hosts.  The latter glory of this house will be greater than the former, says the Lord of hosts, and on this place, I shall give peace, declares the Lord of hosts (Haggai 2:4-9).

From this day on I will bless you (Haggai 2:19b).

But you shall remember the Lord your God for it is He who is given you power to make wealth that He may confirm His covenant.

# Rise to My Defense!

O Lord, oppose those who oppose me. Declare war on those who are attacking me. Put on Your armor, and take up Your shield. Prepare for battle, and come to my aid. Lift up Your spear and javelin and block the way of my enemies. Let me hear You say, "I am your salvation!" Wake up! Rise to my defense! Take up my case, my God and my Lord. Declare me "not guilty," O Lord my God, for You give justice (Psalm 35:1-3, 23,24).

Don't worry about the wicked. Don't envy those who do wrong. For like grass, they soon fade away. Like springtime flowers, they soon wither. Trust in the Lord and do good. Then you will live safely in the land and prosper. Take delight in the Lord, and He will give you your heart's desires. Commit everything you do to the Lord. Trust Him, and He will help you. He will make your innocence as clear as the dawn, and the justice of your cause will shine like the noonday sun. Be still in the presence of the Lord and wait patiently for Him to act. Don't' worry about evil people who prosper or fret about their wicked schemes. Stop your anger!

Turn from your rage!  Do not envy others it only leads to harm. For the wicked will be destroyed, but those who trust the Lord will possess the land.  In a little while, the wicked will disappear.  Though you look for them, they will be gone. Those who are gentle and lowly will possess the land; they will live in prosperous security (Psalm 37:1-11).

For the Lord loves justice, and He will never abandon the godly, He will keep them safe forever (Psalm 37:28).

But the Lord will not let the wicked succeed or let the godly be condemned when they are brought before the judge. Don't be impatient for the Lord to act! Travel steadily along His path.  He will honor you, giving you the land.  You will see the wicked destroyed (Psalm 37:34).

Arise, O LORD!  Deliver me, O my God! Strike all my enemies on the jaw; break the teeth of the wicked (Psalm 3:8).

# Seek the Lord

But first let's ask the Lord for advice (1 Kings:5b).

Seek the Lord while He may be found, call on Him while He is near (Isaiah 55:6).

But if from there you will seek the Lord your God, you will find Him if you seek Him with all your heart and all your soul (Deuteronomy 4:29).

My soul longs for You in the night; indeed, my spirit within me diligently seeks You (Isaiah 26:9)

# Standing on God's Strength

I have strength for all things in Christ, Who empowers me [I am ready for anything and equal to anything through Him Who infuses inner strength into me; I am self-sufficient in Christ's sufficiency] (Philippians 4:13).

When I am pressed on every side by troubles, I am not crushed and broken (2 Corinthians 4:8 TLB).

When I am perplexed because I don't know why things happen as they do, I don't give up and quit (2 Corinthians 4:8).

I do not become discouraged (utterly spiritless, exhausted, and wearied out through fear) (2 Corinthians 4:16-17).

Though my outer man is [progressively] decaying and wasting away, yet my inner self is being [progressively] renewed day after day (2 Corinthians 4:6).

For my light, momentary afflictions (this slight distress of the passing hour) is ever more and more abundantly preparing and producing and achieving for me an everlasting weight of glory [beyond all measure, excessively surpassing all comparisons and all calculation, a vast and transcendent glory and blessedness never to cease!] (2 Corinthians 4:17).

God comforts, encourages and consoles me in every trouble. He enables me to console others who need comfort (2 Corinthians 1:4).

And it shall come to pass in that day, that his burdens shall be taken away from off thy shoulders, and his yoke from off thy neck, and the yoke shall be destroyed because of the anointing (Isaiah 10: 27 KJV).

That he may grant you according to the riches of His glory, to be strengthened with power through His Spirit in the inner man (Ephesians 3:16).

Put on the new self who is being renewed to a true knowledge according to the image of the One who created him (Colossians 3:10).

And let the peace of Christ rule in your hearts, to which indeed you were called in one body; and be thankful. Let the Word of Christ dwell within you (Colossians 3:15-16a).

I urge you therefore, brethren, by the mercies of God, to present your bodies a living and holy sacrifice, acceptable to God which is your spiritual service of worship. And do not be conformed to this world, but be transformed by the renewing of your mind, that you may prove what is the will of God is, that which is good and acceptable and perfect (Romans 12:1).

In the day when I cried out, You answered me, And made me bold with strength in my soul (Psalm 138:3 NKJV).

My grace (My favor and loving-kindness and mercy) is enough for you [sufficient against any danger and enables you to bear the trouble manfully]; for My strength and power are made perfect (fulfilled and completed) and show themselves most effective in [your] weakness. Therefore, I will all the more gladly glory in my weaknesses and infirmities, that the strength and power of Christ (the Messiah) may rest (yes, may He pitch a tent over and all dwell) upon me (2 Corinthians 12:9)!

Yet those who wait for the Lord will gain new strength; They will mount up with wings like eagles, they will run and not get tired, they will walk and not become weary (Isaiah 40: 31).

Do not fear, for I am with you; Do not anxiously look about you, for I am your God (Isaiah 41:10).

# Strength

… but he found strength in the Lord his God (1 Samuel 30: 6c).

He became stronger and stronger because the Lord All-Powerful was with him (2 Samuel 5:10).

The eyes of the Lord go around looking in all the earth for people who are faithful to him so that he can make them strong (1 Chronicles 16:9).

The Lord has redeemed my life from all distress (2 Samuel 4:9).

I cry out to the Lord and He heals me (Psalm 30:2).

The Lord forgives all my sins and heals all my diseases (Psalm 103:3).

He sends His Word and heals me and rescues me from the pit and destruction (Psalm 107:20).

He heals my broken heart and binds up my wounds, curing my pains and sorrows (Psalm 147:3).

The Lord has declared that He will restore me to health and heal my wounds (Jeremiah 30:17).

For you Lord have been a defense for the helpless, a defense for the needy in his distress, a refuge from the storm, a shade from the heat (Isaiah 25:4).

And the Lord God will wipe tears away from all faces, and He will remove the reproach of His people from all the earth; for the Lord has spoken (Isaiah 25:8).

You will guard me and keep me in perfect and constant peace because my mind is stayed on You, because I commit myself to You, I lean on and hope confidently in You. So, I trust in the Lord, I commit myself to You and lean on You, hoping confidently in You forever; for You Lord are the everlasting Rock (Isaiah 26:3-4).

The Lord earnestly waits expecting, looking, and longing to be gracious to you; and therefore, He lifts Himself up, that He may have mercy on me and show loving-kindness to me. For the Lord is a God of justice. Blessed, happy, fortunate and to be envied am I because I wait for Him, and I expect and look and long for His victory, His favor, His love, His peace, His joy, and His matchless, unbroken companionship (Isaiah 30:18).

I will weep no longer.  He will surely be gracious to me and at the sound of my cry, when He hears it He will answer me (Isaiah 30:19).

And my ears will hear a word behind me saying, "This is the way, walk in it," whenever you turn to the right or to the left (Isaiah 30:21).

I hear the Lord, He speaks to me and I know His voice.

Everlasting joy is upon my head.  I will find gladness and joy, and sorrow and sighing will flee away (Isaiah 35:10).

The Everlasting God, the Lord, the Creator of the ends of the earth does not become weary or tired.  His understanding is inscrutable.  He gives strength to the weary, and to him who lacks might He increases power.  Though youths grow weary and tired, and vigorous young men stumble badly, yet those who wait on the Lord will gain new strength; they will mount up with wings like eagles, they will run and not get tired, they will walk and not become weary (Isaiah 40:28-31).

You are My servant, I have chosen you.  Do not fear, for I am with you; do not anxiously look about you, for I am your God.  I will strengthen you, surely, I will help you, surely, I will uphold you with My righteous right hand (Isaiah 41:9-10).

But now, thus says the Lord, your creator, and He who formed you, do not fear, for I have redeemed you; I have called you by name; you are Mine!  When you pass through the waters I will be with you; and through the rivers they will not overflow you.  When you walk through the fire, you will not be scorched, nor will the flame burn you.  For I am the Lord your God, the Holy One of Israel, your Savior…You are precious in My sight, you are honored by Me and I love you… do not fear, for I am with you (Isaiah 43:1-7).

Behold, I will do something new, now it will spring forth; will you not be aware of it?  I will even make a road way in the wilderness and rivers in the desert (Isaiah 43:19).

I will go before you and make the rough places smooth… I will give you the treasures of darkness, and hidden wealth of secret places, in order that you may know that it is I, the Lord, the God of Israel who calls you by name… My chosen one, I have also called you by your name; I have given you a title of honor (Isaiah 45:2-4).

I, even I, am He who comforts you (Isaiah 51:12).

For the Lord will go ahead of me and the God of Israel will protect me from behind.  Behold My servant will prosper, he will be high and lifted up and greatly exalted (Isaiah 52:12-13).

I will have a multitude of (spiritual) children and heirs.  I will enjoy a long life, and the Lord's plan will prosper in my hands (Isaiah 53:10).

My loving-kindness will not be removed from you and My covenant of peace will not be shaken, says the Lord who has compassion on you (Isaiah 54:10).

For the rain and the snow come down from heaven, and stay on the ground to water the earth.  They cause the grain to grow, producing seed for the farmer and bread for the hungry.  It is the same with my Word.  I will send it out, and it always produces fruit.  It will accomplish all I want it to, and it will prosper everywhere I send it.  You will live in joy and peace (Isaiah 55:10-12).

I will lead them and comfort those who mourn.  Then words of praise will be on their lips.  May they have peace; both near and far, for I will heal them all, says the Lord (Isaiah 57:18-19).

Arise from the depression and prostration in which circumstances have kept you – rise to a new life! Shine, and be radiant with the glory of the Lord, for your light has come, and the glory of the Lord has risen upon you… The Lord shall arise upon you and His glory shall be seen on you…. Then you shall see and be radiant and your heart shall thrill and tremble with joy at the glorious deliverance and be enlarged; because the abundant wealth of the Dead Sea shall be turned to you, unto you shall the nations come with their treasures (Isaiah 60:1-5).

I have been given a garland of beauty instead of ashes, and I have been given the oil of joy instead of mourning, and the garment of expressive praise instead of a heavy, burdened, and failing spirit – so I might be called oaks of righteousness. (I am lofty, strong, and magnificent; I am distinguished for uprightness, justice and right standing with God) (Isaiah 61:3).

Instead of shame I will have a double portion, and instead of humiliation I will shout for joy over my portion. Therefore, I will possess double portion in my land, everlasting joy will be mine, for you Lord love justice, and hate robbery in the burnt offering; you will faithfully give me my recompense, and you will make an everlasting covenant with me. And my offspring will be known among the nations and my descendants in the midst of the peoples. All who see me and my children will recognize me because we are the offspring whom the Lord has blessed (Isaiah 61:7-9).

But now, O Lord, You are my Father, and I am the clay, and you are the Potter; and I am the work of Your hand (Isaiah 64:8).

# Successful

The Lord was with Hezekiah, so he was successful in everything he did (2 Kings 18:6).

Jabez prayed to the God of Israel and said, "I pray that you would bless me and give me more land!  Be near me and don't let anyone hurt me!  Then I will not have any pain. God gave Jabez what he asked for (2 Chronicles 4:10).

Have faith in the Lord your God, and you will stand strong! … and you will succeed (2 Chronicles 20:20b)!

Uzziah was obeying the Lord, God gave him success.  (2 Chronicles 26:6).

# Successful in All I Do

God has made me successful in everything (Genesis 41:51).

Don't be afraid.  I am with you, and I will bless you.  I will make your family great.  The Lord blessed him very much. Isaac became rich.  He gathered more and more wealth until he became a very rich man (Genesis 26:12b-13).

Now it is clear that the Lord has blessed you. (Genesis 26:29).

You are the God Who Sees Me… I see that even in this place God sees me and cares for me (Genesis 16:13).

But is anything too hard for the Lord (Genesis 18:14)?

# Suicide

Why must a suffering person continue to live?  Why let anyone live such a bitter life?  Such people want to die, but death does not come.  They search for death more than hidden treasure.  They would be happy to find their grave. They would rejoice to find their tomb.  But God keeps their future a secret and builds a wall around them to protect them (Job 3:20-23).

He will save you again and again.  No evil will harm you. God will save you from death when there is famine (Job 5:19-20).

At just the right time we will reap a harvest of blessings if we don't give up (Galatians 6:9).

Don't give up when He corrects you (Hebrews 12:5).

# The Reward of the Wicked

Evil people might look for help, but they will not escape their troubles.  Their hope leads only to death (Job 11:20).

He (God) exposes even the darkest secrets (Job 12:22).

And they said that an evil man suffers all his life.  A cruel man suffers all his numbered years.  Every noise scares him. His enemy will attack him when he thinks he is safe.  An evil man has no hope of escaping the darkness.  There is a sword somewhere waiting to kill him.  He wanders from place to place looking for food.  But he knows a darkness is coming, which he brought on himself.  He lives in fear, with worrying and suffering threatening him like a king ready to attack. That is because that evil man shook his fist at God, refusing to obey.  He dared to attack God All-Powerful (Job 15:20-25).

Here is what God has planned for those who are evil.  This is what cruel people will get from God All-Powerful… Evil people collect silver as easily as dirt.  They may have so many clothes that they are piled up like clay.  But their piles of clothes will be worn by those who have lived right.  All that silver will be given to those who have done no wrong.  Evil people might build houses, but they will not last long.  They will be like a spider's web or a guard's ten.  They might be rich when they go to bed, but when they open their eyes, all their riches will be gone.  Terrible "fears will come over them like a flood, like a storm in the night that blows everything away.  The east wind will carry them away, and they will be gone.  The storm will sweep them out of their homes.  They may try to run away from the power of the storm, but it will come down on them without mercy… (Job 27:13-22).

The Lord protects those who do right, but he destroys those who do wrong.  Good people will always be safe, but the wicked will be forced out of the land (Proverbs 10:29-30).

The Lord is with me.  He shows that I am innocent, so no one will be able to show I am guilty.  If someone wants to try to prove I am wrong, that person should come to me, and we will have a trial.  But look, the Lord God helps me, so no one can prove me guilty.  As for them, they will be like worthless old clothes, eaten by moths (Isaiah 50:8-9).

I am the Lord and I love justice.  I hate stealing and everything that is wrong.  So, I will give the people what they deserve.  I will make an agreement with my people forever (Isaiah 61:8).

Then My anger will blaze forth against them (abusers).  I will abandon them, hiding my face from them, and they will be devoured. Terrible trouble will come down on them, and on that day they will say, "These disasters have come down on us because God is no longer with us (Deuteronomy 31:17).

# Verbal Abuse

God saves the poor from the hurtful words of the wicked. He saves them from those who are powerful. So the poor have hope; God shuts the mouths of those who would cause them harm (Job 5:15-16).

God will protect you. You will not be afraid when bad things happen! You will laugh at the destruction and famine. You will not be afraid of wild animals! It is as if you have a peace treaty with the wild animals and the rocks in the field. You will live in peace because your tent is safe. You will count your property and find nothing missing (Job 5:21-24).

The Lord God will help me, so the bad things they say will not hurt me. I will be strong. I know I will not be disappointed (Isaiah 50:7 ERV).

People will make weapons to fight against you, but their weapons will not defeat you. Some people will say things against you, but anyone who speaks against you will be proved worn. In the past, other people shamed you and said bad things to you. You were shamed much more than any other people. So in your land you will get two times more than other people.  You will get the joy that continues forever.  That's because I am the Lord and I love justice.  I hate stealing and everything that is wrong.  So I will give the people what they deserve.  I will make an agreement with my people forever (Isaiah 61:7-8).


Lord, you have seen my troubles.  Now judge my case for me. You have seen how my enemies have hurt me.  You have seen all the evil plans that they made against me.  You heard them insult me, Lord.  You have heard all the evil plans made against me.  The words and thought of my enemies are against me all the time – when they sit down and when they stand up.  Look how they make fun of me!  Give them back what they deserve, Lord.  Pay them back for what they've done.  Make them stubborn and then curse them.  Chase them in anger and destroy them.  Wipe them off the face of the earth, Lord (Lamentations 3: 59-66).

# Victory

The Lord gave victory to David wherever he went (2 Samuel 7:6).

You will win the battle.  The Lord will let you defeat them (2 Chronicles 18:11b).

Victory comes from the Lord; may He bless His people (Psalm 3:8).

Arise, O Lord! Deliver me, O my God! … Salvation belongs to the Lord; may Your blessing be on Your people.  Selah (Psalm 3:7-8).

# Vindicate Me

Vindicate me, declare me innocent O Lord, for I have acted with integrity. (Psalm 26:1).

Turn to me and have mercy on me, for I am alone and in deep distress. My problems go from bad to worse. Oh, save me from them all! Feel my pain and see my trouble. See how many enemies I have and how viciously they hate me! Protect me! Rescue my life from them! Do not let me be disgraced, for I trust in you (Psalm 25: 16-20).

Hear me my beloved, do not be faint hearted. Do not be afraid, or panic or tremble before them. For I, the Lord your God is the one who goes with you to fight for you and against your enemies to save you (Deuteronomy 20:3).

For I have said do not touch my anointed ones, and you my beloved are My anointed (1 Chronicles 16:22).

For when you are helpless I am your defense, I will defend you in your need and in your distress; I am your refuge in the storm (Isaiah 25:4).

For I the Lord will administer justice every morning; and deliver you from your oppressor (Jeremiah 21:12).

Behold I am going to send and angel before you to guard you along the way and bring you into the place which I have prepared (Exodus 23:20).

And do not for a moment be frightened or intimidated in anything by your opponents and adversaries, for such fearlessness will be a clear sign to them of their pending destruction and sure evidence of your deliverance and salvation that comes from Me (Philippians 1:28).

Do not fear them for the Lord your God is the one fighting for you (Deuteronomy 3:22).

My presence shall go with you and I will give you rest (Exodus 33:13).\

I have created you and have cared for you since before you were born. I will be your God throughout your lifetime – until your hair is white with age. I made you, and I will care for you. I will care you along and save you (Isaiah 46:3-4).

I am with you in all you do (Genesis 21:22).

I will provide for you (Genesis 22:14).

Do not fear for I am a shield to you (Genesis 15:1).

You will be singing songs of everlasting joy. Sorrow and mourning will disappear and you will be overcome with joy and gladness. I will come and do for you all the good things I have promised, and will bring you home again. For I know the plans I have for you, they are for good and not for disaster, to give you a future and a hope (Jeremiah 29:10-11).

# What About My Children?

That's because I will fight your battles, and I will save your children (Isaiah 49:25).

Your children will all be followers of God.  And they will have real peace (Isaiah 54:13).

And they shall put My name upon the children of Israel; and I will bless them (Numbers 6:27).

And He will love thee, and bless thee, and multiply thee: He will also bless thy children (Deuteronomy 7:31).

For the Lord will bless their children and their descendants (Isaiah 65:23).

# When I Feel Like I'm Drowning

The Lord reached down from above and grabbed me.   He pulled me from the deep water.   He saved me from my powerful enemies who hated me.  They were too strong for me, so He saved me.  They attacked me in my time of trouble but the Lord was there to support me.  He was pleased with me, so He rescued me.  He took me to a safe place (2 Samuel 22:17-20).

The Lord is close to those who have suffered disappointment.  He saves those who are discouraged (Psalm 34:18).

God is our refuge and strength, a very present help in trouble (Psalm 46:1).

The Lord sees what happens everywhere, He watches everyone, good and evil (Proverbs 15:3).

# Why You Don't Have to Worry

*You never have to worry about what happened to you, because God has seen it and He will NOT let the guilty go unpunished. That is His promise to you.*

Turn to the Lord for help in everything you do, and you will be successful. The Lord has a plan for everything. In His plan, the wicked will be destroyed (2 Kings 18:6).

Don't worry – I am with you. Don't be afraid – I am your God. I will make you strong. I will help you. I will support you with my right hand that brings victory. Look, some people are angry with you, but they will be ashamed and disgraced. Your enemies will be lost and disappear. You will look for the people who were against you, but you will not be able to find them. Those who fought against you will disappear completely (Isaiah 41:10-12).

So don't remember what happened in earlier times.  Don't think about what happened a long time ago, because I am doing something new!  Now you will grow like a new plant.  Surely you will know this is true (Isaiah 43:18-19).

*Although you've had a rough past, God is saying you don't need to think about it anymore, actually, STOP thinking about it, because He has something wonderful for you!*

When I make a promise, that promise is true.  It will happen (Isaiah 45:23).

*Every word in the Bible is God's promise to you.  God is saying these Scripture are My promise to you and it will happen.*

In the same way, My Words leave my mouth, and they don't come back without results.  My Words make the things happen that I want to happen.  They succeed in doing what I send them to do (Isaiah 55:11 ERV).

The troubles of the past will be forgotten.  No one will remember them.  My people will be happy ad rejoice forever because of what I will make it (Isaiah 65:17b-18).

Who can stand before His indignation who can endure the burning of His anger?  His wrath is poured out like fire, and the rocks are broken up by Him.  The Lord is good, a strong hold in the day of trouble, and He knows those who take refuge in Him. But with an overflowing flood He will make a complete end of its site, and will pursue His enemies into darkness (Nahum 1:6-8).

# Wisdom

He had the wisdom of God to make the right decisions

(1 Kings 3:28b).

Prayer: I don't have the wisdom to make sound decisions, Lord help me know now the difference between right and wrong. Without such wisdom I cannot do what you desire for me (1 Kings 3:7-9).

Wisdom will save you from the ways of the wicked men (Proverbs 2:12).

Walk in all the ways that the Lord your God has commanded (Deuteronomy 5:33).

# Healing Scripture
# Psalm 23

Are you looking to find a healing Scripture that captures your heart, fills the void; restore hope; remind you everything will be okay; one that will give you encouragement and hope again?  That healing Scripture is found in Psalm 23.  The Psalm 23 provides us with a rich resource of God's goodness.   It's full of His loving tenderness – It's His master plan for our lives.

The Lord is my Shepherd – that's a Relationship!

I shall not want – that's Supply!

He makes me to lie down in green pastures – that's Rest!

He leads me beside the still waters – that's Refreshment!

He restores my soul – that's Healing!

He leads me in the paths of righteousness – that's Guidance!

For His name's sake – that's Purpose!

Yea, though I walk through the valley of the shadow of death – that's Testing!

I will fear no evil – that's Protection!

For are with me – that's Faithfulness!

Thy rod and Thy staff comfort me – that's Discipline!

You prepare a table before me in the presence of mine enemies – that's Hope!

Thou anoint my head with oil – that's Consecration!

My cup runs over – that's Abundance!

Surely goodness and mercy shall follow me all the days of my life –- that's Blessing!

And I will dwell in the house of the Lord – that's Security!

Forever – that's Eternity!

 What is most valuable is not what we have in our lives, but WHO we have in our lives.

# About the Author

Kelly Ann Evers is an author of 46 books, 100's of published articles, owner of The Dry Skin Experts, and founder of the His Love Heals, Domestic Violence Help Organization.  She is a serial student with two master's degrees from SCBC and The King's University, as well as, an unknown number of units from UCLA and UC Davis and WV University.  She has two beautiful children and one grandchild.  Newest on her wish list, is to travel to Panama to help at a sloth rehabilitation center.

Her mission is to motivate women through Prayer and the Word of God by empowering, encouraging, and inspiring them to succeed.

Learn more about Kelly at:

www.Facebook.com/kellyannevers

# More About Kelly

It's our pleasure to introduce Kelly Ann Evers. Kelly is a published author, victims' advocate, authority and consultant on domestic violence issues, and the founder of His Love Heals, Domestic Violence Help™ an international organization headquartered in Southern California that is based on biblical principles.

His Love Heals, Domestic Violence Help™ provides resources to 200 countries and in 80 languages to women, pastors, community leaders, and service organizations. As a survivor of severe domestic violence and sexual abuse, and through the extraordinary, transformed life God has given her, Kelly's mission is to bring healing, help, and hope to battered and abused women by empowering, encouraging, and inspiring them to succeed.

Known for her loving spirit, wisdom, and compassion, Kelly draws upon her own painful past, and remarkable healing, as she leads battered and abused women toward achieving the bright and beautiful future they deserve.

She helps them find the strength to put one foot in front of the other, and she teaches them to never give up or settle for anything less than God's perfect plan for them. With her guidance, women throughout this world have learned to trust God with all their concerns, and to soar above life's often overwhelming trials by tapping into His strength through prayer and the Word of God.

Defining moment: Kelly recalls that the defining moment in her life occurred on October 10, 2001. It was the day God spoke directly to her. He told her that He would heal her. At that time she was suffering with PTSD, brain trauma and amnesia from her husband's last beatings, severe depression, and emotional scars from years of abuse. She wanted to end her life. God's words to her gave her hope for the first time. She realized from that moment on that she was a child of God, and that there was a purpose to her life. She never again saw herself as a battered woman who dared not to dream. For the first time in her life, she knew what it was like to feel God's love. It was life-changing.

Information about Domestic Violence: One out of every three women in our nation and one out of every four women in our churches will become victims of domestic violence during their lifetime. Women who are living through the nightmare of domestic abuse, or their friends and family who want to help them, are reaching out in desperation for answers.

In her new books, "Dynamic Prayers, Changed Lives,"

**and**
"Creating Your Personal Safety Plan:
Domestic Violence Emergency Planning Kit"

Kelly Ann Evers gives victims of abuse the tools to safely and successfully escape from their abusers, and shows them how to find peace, healing, hope, and comfort through prayer and the Word of God.

Education and Expertise: Academically, and in the field, Kelly has spent the last two decades researching how abuse can affect women on every level of their lives, and she uses her vast knowledge and personal experience to teach and encourage women to heal from the ill effects of abuse, and to live fulfilling, happy lives.

Additionally, she has invested over a decade studying the psychological profiles of batterers, their behavioral patterns, and their recovery and healing. Her notable "Batterer Intervention Program" used by pastors and community leaders, helps rehabilitate batterers and abusers.

Kelly has two Master's Degree at The Kings University and Southern California Bible College. She is a proud mother of two, and a grandmother of one.

# *Other Books by Kelly*

## A Thousand Scriptures Series:

- A Thousand Scriptures: God's Word on Domestic Violence … because love should never hurt! (Series 1)

- A Thousand Scriptures: Scriptures Only   (Series 2)

- A Thousand Scriptures: Another 1000 Scriptures on Domestic Violence (Series 3)

- A Thousand Scriptures Pastor's Edition    (Series 4)

## Why Does He Keep Hurting Me?

- Why Does He Keep Hurting Me?  Questions Everyone Wants to Know; What You Need to Know about Domestic Violence and Domestic Abuse before It's Too Late

## Create A Safety Plan:

- Create A Safety Plan:
  Domestic Violence Emergency Planning Kit

## Domestic Violence Sucks:

- Domestic Violence Sucks: Journaling Each Incident: 28 Intentional Questions that Keep A Record of Everything He's Done.

## God's Love Heals Everywhere You Hurt: S.T.A.M.P. Scripture Journal:

- God's Love
- Justice God's Way!
- Heal from Abuse
- Anxiety and Fear
- God Will Fight for You!

## God's Word on Domestic Violence:

- God's Word on Domestic Violence: One Thousand Scriptures on Abuse… because love should never hurt!  (Series 1)

- God's Word on Domestic Violence: Scriptures Only (Series 2)

- God's Word on Domestic Violence: Another 1000 Scriptures on Domestic Violence (Series 3)

- God's Word on Domestic Violence: Pastor's Edition    (Series 4)

## Dynamic Prayers, Changed Lives Series:

- Dynamic Prayers, Changed Lives: One Woman's Journey of Healing from Abuse… through Prayer and the Word of God

- Dynamic Prayers, Changed Lives… Prayer Journal and Coloring Book

- Dynamic Scriptures, Changed Lives… Prayer Journal and Coloring Book

## Dynamic Prayers, Changed Lives Kindle Series:

- Dynamic Prayers, Changed Lives: One Woman's Journey of Healing from Abuse… through Prayer and the Word of God

- Dynamic Prayers, Changed Lives… Prayer Journal and Coloring Book

- Dynamic Scriptures, Changed Lives… Prayer Journal and Coloring Book

# Names of God Series:

## Names of God: Prayer Journal Adult Coloring Book (Series 1)

- Choose Between:
  - Style: Thick Black and White Doodle Art (Series (1a)
  - Style: Fun and Whimsical Art (Series (1b)
  - Style: Picturesque Global Landmarks (Series (1c)
  - Style: Beautiful Butterflies (Series (1d)
  - Style: Zentangle Sea Life (Series (1e)
  - Style: Blank Background for Personalized Doodling (1f)

## Names of God: Prayer Journal Adult Coloring Book (Series 2)

- Choose Between:

  - Style: Birds, Peacocks and Owls (2a)
  - Style: Exquisite Flowers (2b)
  - Style: Hand-Drawn Mandala Doodles (2c)

- o Style: Blank Background for Personalized Doodling (2d)

## Names of God: Prayer Journal Adult Coloring Book (Series 3)

- Choose Between:

    - o Style: Sweet, Savory, and Other Yummy Treats! (3a)
    - o Style: Cats, Dogs, and Other Pet Friends (3b)
    - o Style: Lions, Tigers, and Bears and Other Zoo Animals (3c)
    - o Style: Delightful Hand-Drawn Cats (3d)
    - o Style: Adorable Hand-Drawn Dogs (3e)
    - o Style: Blank Background for Personalized Doodling (3f)

## Names of God: Prayer Journal Adult Coloring Book (Series 4, Hebrew Names)

- Choose Between:

    - o Style: Easy Hand-Drawn Mandala Patterns (4a)
    - o Style: Ornate Hand-Drawn Zentangle Art (4b)
    - o Style: Easy Thick Black and White Doodles (4c)

- Style: Blank Background for Personalized Doodling (4d)

## The Perfect Skin Detox Series:

- The Perfect Skin Detox: Gorgeous Skin in 10 Days or Less

- The Perfect Skin Detox: Easy-to-Make Juice Recipes

- The Perfect Skin Detox: Simple Artistic Salads-To-Go

## The Perfect Skin Detox Journal Series:

- The Perfect Skin Detox: Journal Coloring Book

  - Hand-Sketched Zentangle Fruit and Vegetable

## God's Name, God's Power! Series:

- God's Love, God's Power! Journal Coloring Book

- God's Peace, God's Power! Journal Coloring Book

- God's Name, God's Power! Journal Coloring Book

- God's Joy, God's Power! Journal Coloring Book

- God's Hope, God's Power! Journal Coloring Book

God's Healing, God's Power! Journal Coloring Book

# One Last Thing

If you enjoyed this book, I'd be very grateful if you'd post a short (or long!) review on Amazon. Your support really does make a difference. I personally read all the reviews. Your comments encourage me to write more and know what you want in the future.

Thanks again for your support!

Kelly Ann Evers

# Start Reading two of Kelly's Newest Books

## Why Does He Keep Hurting Me?  Questions Everyone Wants to Know



## Dynamic Prayers Changed Lives: One Woman's Journey of Healing from Abuse through Prayer and Scriptures

# Excerpt from:

# Why Does He Keep Hurting Me?
# Questions Everyone Wants to Know

# Chapter 4: The Mind of the Batterer

Who are these men, so captivating, so attractive, so intriguing and magnetic, they have the ability to charm their way into everyone's heart, and whose charisma is so mesmerizing that you long for your own husband to possess their qualities?  They are doctors, lawyers, school teachers, police officers, garbage men and executives.  They are your next-door neighbor, your bank teller, your grocery store clerk and even your brother-in-law.

They come from all walks of life. They're in affluent neighborhoods and in underprivileged neighborhoods. They are Anglo, Hispanic, Asian, African American and every other nationality. How are they so appealing in social settings people swarm to them, yet internally they are a sweltering volcano?

How can he be at the office giving a dynamic presentation or entertaining at lunch with co-workers or friends, then in a split second he turns vicious and beats his wife mercilessly? How can he be cheering at a baseball game or even playing with the children at the park then drive home 30 minutes later then stab his wife repeatedly? How is he able to deceive co-workers, family, friends and even his wife?

As a victim of severe spousal abuse, I questioned this myself. I wondered how in my own situation that I could spend twenty years enduring horrific torture, yet remain in the situation. During the last eight years of my marriage, I spent endless hours trying to find a way of escape from a man who would not let me go.

To the world, I lived a beautiful life with a perfect home, perfect children, perfect husband and perfect businesses. However, behind the four walls of our home, I lived a secret life of grotesque violence. Nevertheless, not only was the world deceived – but so was I.

I sought those years understanding what abuse is, and why I allowed him to instill that fear, that hopelessness, that deceptiveness and that inability to leave. To understand why a woman would endure such torture, you would have to understand the mind of a batterer.

Domestic violence is a silent crime, so shocking, so horrific, that it's swept under the rug as if it doesn't exist. A world so terrifying, that when women cry for help from family, friends, police and even our judicial system – they find no comfort.

The courts and police don't see batterers that injure their wife as a serious crime. Regardless of the victim's wounds, the courts hardly punish with severe consequences; and the police dismiss it as a domestic dispute.

Then to make matters worse, even though the batterer broke her bones, mangled her face, bruised beyond recognition, the batterer will claim she attacked him and it was self-defense. Now the wife goes to jail while the batterer goes free, once again.

When this type of event happens repeatedly, and the wife goes back to jail for the abuse done to her, the husband will tell his wife if she tries to leave, she will lose her kids. This kind of intimidation works, because no mother will leave her children behind with an angry violent man.

Even more unfortunate, friends and families fear involving themselves because of the possibility of endangering their own lives. And many times, they also believe the batterer is the victim.

Without hope, they continue to endure years of horrifying beatings. They are alone to suffer the unspeakable pain, tormenting fears, and a multitude of abuse. In rare cases of escape, many remain physically and emotionally damaged and some unable to live normal lives.

Horribly worse, these women live in daily fear knowing that the abuser may be stalking them. Friends and family and associates are shocked when a woman exposes the truth of the horrendous abuse she endured for years, maybe even decades.

Family and friends who know both the husband and wife are shocked in disbelief when the truth of their friends has ruthlessly beaten his wife for incompressible reasons.

I spent about ten years trying to escape. He always found me. Always. I went out of state, I paid only cash so he couldn't track me by check or charge. It wasn't until I escaped for the last time my mechanic found a tracking device on my car.

Finding the tracking device… to finish reading this book please order: Why Does He Keep Hurting Me? Questions Everyone Wants to Know; Knowing What You Need to Know about Domestic Violence and Domestic Abuse before It's Too Late

# Excerpt from:

# Dynamic Prayers, Changed Lives

# Chapter 1: Putting on a Façade

No one really knew me. I was extremely skillful at putting on a façade. I lived a prestigious life filled with wealth and travel, and I was quite aware that many people were envious of me. *If they only knew.* Outwardly, I appeared to be a beautiful woman who had the perfect husband, the perfect children, the perfect home, but behind the walls of our house, my children and I inhabited a world filled with fear and violence.

After the birth of my daughter, my husband's drinking had escalated, and so did his violence toward me. For years I felt all alone, believing it was my lot in life for my husband to physically, emotionally, and spiritually abuse me. My marriage had become my prison. Unknown to me, there was even a tracking device on my car so my husband constantly knew where I went.

He was never going to let me leave.

I had run away from him numerous times, taking our children with me, but he always found us, and forced me to return to him. I had lost all hope, my self-worth had been beaten out of me, and I was completely numb inside. I often would dream of the day when I successfully escaped from my husband. I knew, or at least I imagined it would be true, that once I left him, my life would be perfect, happy, and peaceful.

On April 7, 2001 my husband beat me so severely that I suffered an acute head injury. I was supposed to take his car to the car wash that day, one of my weekly chores, so we had exchanged keys earlier. After assaulting me, he left the house in my car. He had just viciously attacked me, I was clearly injured, but he still expected me to get his car washed later that day! My young daughter and I went on automatic pilot, refusing to give into the fear and terror we felt. We knew we didn't have much time to get out of the house before he returned.

As I threw our belongings into suitcases, I realized I had no idea where we were going, what our future held, or if he would find us. Nothing would ever be the same. We might be forced to live well – below the poverty line on a peanut butter and crackers diet, without any of the luxuries we were used to having. But my daughter and I didn't care. We wanted freedom from him, freedom from fear and terror, freedom from abuse.

My son was away at private school so I knew he would be safe. I loaded up my husband's car and told my daughter to make one last run through the house to see if she wanted anything else. I held my dog for what I thought would be the last time, and as my tears soaked her soft, white fur, I whispered, "I love you."

My daughter came down the stairs with her arms full of stuffed animals and a book. We stood for a second, glancing quickly around our house, at the life we were leaving behind. I said, "Let's go," and led her to the car.

I found a secluded area outside a library that was two cities from our home, parked the car, and I stopped to catch my breath. My daughter and I sat quietly, staring out the windows. I felt paralyzed. With shaking hands and a quivering voice, I called the battered women's shelter. A soft, gentle voice, calm and reassuring, let me know that everything would be okay. She set a time and place to meet.

When she saw me, she noticed that I was suffering from a serious head injury and insisted that I needed to go to the emergency room.  I ended up being hospitalized for two weeks. Once I was out of the hospital, my daughter and I entered the battered women's shelter and were given a room with bunk beds.

My daughter took the top bunk, I took the bottom. The moment I put my head on the pillow I began to cry, and for the next three days the tears that I had held inside for years came pouring out of me.

In my mind, I had pictured battered women's shelters as depressing, dark, dreary places where hundreds of profoundly sad women and children stood side by side, weeping uncontrollably, packed together like farm animals. They had no hope, no future.

We entered a completely different reality.  The shelter was a beautiful home with everything women and their children would want or need. The women I met there were happy and optimistic.

The shelter didn't just provide food and housing. It gave women hope for the future and assisted us with our legal documents and our court hearings. It helped with our clothing, makeup, medical needs, therapy, jobs, and so much more.

As we settled into our new home, my daughter and I began group, individual, and family therapy. The therapist was sharp, creative, and knew domestic violence well. Between daily therapy, making plans for our future, and preparing for court, two weeks passed quickly.

Our court date arrived, and the shelter's advocate assured me that everything would work out fine. She was right. My husband was ordered to provide financial support for my daughter and me, a restraining order was granted, and I also obtained a Kick Out Order. My husband had 15 minutes to remove his belongings. My daughter and I were going to be able to return to our home!

After packing our belongings and cleaning the room for the next guest, we left the shelter, and headed home. I was terrified that my husband might be hiding in the house so I had the police meet us there. We were relieved to be reunited with our beloved dog, and to be back in our home.

Looking back on that time now, I realize that if it hadn't been car wash day when I received my last beating from my husband, I would have escaped in my own car, and the tracking device that my husband had secretly installed would have allowed him to find my daughter and me quickly.

I like to think that God was cheering me on that spring day in 2001 as I successfully made my get away from my husband in my husband's own vehicle! … to finish reading this book please order: Dynamic Prayers, Changed Lives:

One Woman's Journey of Healing from Abuse... through Prayer and the Word of God

www.ingramcontent.com/pod-product-compliance
Lightning Source LLC
Chambersburg PA
CBHW061254120726

48001CB00001B/306